GCSE 9-1

geography

OCR B

Exam Practice

Series editor
Bob Digby   **Nicholas Rowles**

OXFORD
UNIVERSITY PRESS

OXFORD
UNIVERSITY PRESS

Great Clarendon Street, Oxford, OX2 6DP, United Kingdom

Oxford University Press is a department of the University of Oxford.
It furthers the University's objective of excellence in research, scholarship,
and education by publishing worldwide. Oxford is a registered trade mark of
Oxford University Press in the UK and in certain other countries

Series editor: Bob Digby

Authors: Bob Digby and Nicholas Rowles

The moral rights of the authors have been asserted.

Database right of Oxford University Press (maker) 2019.

First published in 2019

British Library Cataloguing in Publication Data
Data available

ISBN 978-019-843609-6

10 9 8 7 6 5

Paper used in the production of this book is a natural, recyclable product made
from wood grown in sustainable forests. The manufacturing process conforms
to the environmental regulations of the country of origin.

Printed and bound by CPI Group (UK) Ltd, Croydon, CR0 4YY

Acknowledgements

The publisher and authors would like to thank the following for permission to
use photographs and other copyright material:

Cover: Rob Hyrons/Shutterstock; **p16:** RomeoFox/Alamy Stock Photo; **p23:**
Minden Pictures/Alamy Stock Photo; **p31:** Bob Digby; **p47:** Sanja Sparica/
Alamy Stock Photo; **p120:** ssuaphotos/Shutterstock; **p120:** M. Shcherbyna/
Shutterstock, pajtica/Shutterstock, Catmando/Shutterstock, Creative Nature
Media/Shutterstock, Kletr/Shutterstock, trialhuni/Shutterstock, Janelle Lugge/
Shutterstock; **p121:** wonganan/iStockphoto; **p128:** © Jeff Morgan 04/Alamy
Stock Photo; **p127:** Courtesy of Leese and Nagle; **p137, 160:** Ordnance Survey
© Crown copyright and Database rights 2019.; **p138(t):** pjhpix/Shutterstock;
p138(b): pjhpix/Shutterstock; **p140(t):** © Robert Stainforth/Alamy Stock
Photo; **p140(m):** Uknip/Alamy Stock Photo; **p140(b):** Allan Devlin/Alamy Stock
Photo; **p141:** Andy Sutton/Alamy Stock Photo; **p142:** Angela Hampton Picture
Library/Alamy Stock Photo; **p143:** timsimages/Alamy Stock Photo; **p150(t):**
Realimage/Alamy Stock Photo; **p150(b):** David Pimborough/Alamy Stock Photo;
p152: SMETEK/SCIENCE PHOTO LIBRARY; **p153:** Accent Alaska.com/Alamy
Stock Photo; **p154:** John Giles /PA Archive/PA Images; **p156:** Brian Kinney/
Shutterstock; **p159(t):** Chumash Maxim/Shutterstock; **p159(b):** by sharaff/Getty
Images.

Artwork by Aptara Inc, Mike Connor, Barking Dog Art, Simon Tegg, Kamae
Design, Lovell Johns, Mike Parsons, Q2A Media Services Inc.

Every effort has been made to contact copyright holders of material reproduced
in this book. Any omissions will be rectified in subsequent printings if notice is
given to the publisher.

Guided answers and mark schemes are
available at **www.oxfordsecondary.co.uk/geography-answers**.

Please note: The Practice Paper exam-style questions and mark schemes have not been
written or approved by OCR B. The answers and commentaries provided represent one
interpretation only and other solutions may be appropriate.

Contents

Introduction

How to be successful in your exams

If you want to be successful in your exams, then you need to know how you will be examined, what kinds of questions you will come up against in the exam, how to use what you know and what you will get marks for. That's where this book can help.

How to use this book

This book contains the following features to help you prepare for exams for the OCR GCSE (9-1) in Geography B specification. It is written to work alongside two other OUP publications to support your learning:

- *GCSE 9–1 Geography OCR B Student Book*
- *GCSE 9–1 Geography OCR B Revision Guide*

An introduction (pages 4–13)

This section contains details about:

- the exam papers you'll be taking and what you need to revise
- how exam papers are marked and how to aim for the highest grades.

On your marks (pages 14–65)

This section contains detailed guidance on how to answer questions about specific topics using extended writing for 4, 6, 8 and 12 marks in Papers 1–3.

It also contains space for you to write and assess exam answers so that you get to know how to write good quality, focused responses.

Exam papers (pages 66–159)

This section contains two sets of exam papers. These match the style of those you'll meet in the OCR GCSE Geography B exam. Each set contains:

- Exam Papers 1 and 2, which assess your knowledge and understanding of the course, together with fieldwork in each paper. You'll have undertaken two days of fieldwork to prepare for these questions – one day of physical geography (assessed in Paper 1) and one day of human geography (assessed in Paper 2).
- Exam Paper 3, which consists of a decision-making exercise (often called a DME), applied to an unseen situation. This exam assesses your skill in interpreting a Resource Booklet and your ability to apply your understanding to it.

Each exam paper has space to write answers, with an online mark scheme.

The OCR GCSE (9-1) in Geography B specification has three components. Each component contains specific topics. Each component is assessed by an exam paper (Papers 1, 2 and 3) with sections for different topics, as follows:

Component 1 Our Natural World

This is assessed by Paper 1. It consists of two sections, each on different topics.

- **Section A** consists of questions on four topics (Global Hazards, Changing Climate, Distinctive Landscapes and Sustaining Ecosystems). Each topic has questions worth a total of 13 marks, and the longest question will be worth either 6 or 8 marks. You need to know the examples in the panel on the right.
- **Section B** consists of questions on physical geography fieldwork.

In addition, there are questions assessing your geographical skills (e.g. interpreting statistics, maps, diagrams or photos) and maths skills threaded through each topic.

Memory jogger for Paper 1!

- My case study of a flash flood or tropical storm was of _____ .
- My case study of a heatwave or drought was of _____ .
- My case study of a tectonic event was of _____ .
- My case study of a coastal landscape was of _____ .
- My case study of a river basin was of _____ .
- My case study of attempts to manage an area of rainforest sustainably was of _____ .
- My case study of a small-scale example of sustainable management in the Antarctic or Arctic was of _____ .
- My physical fieldwork was on _____ (name of topic) and we collected data on _____ at (name of place) _____ .

Component 2 People and Society

This is assessed by Paper 2. It consists of two sections, each on different topics.

- **Section A** consists of questions on four topics (Urban Futures, Dynamic Development, UK in the 21st Century and Resource Reliance). Each topic has questions worth a total of 13 marks, and the longest will be worth 6 or 8 marks. See the examples on the right.
- **Section B** consists of questions on human geography fieldwork.

Like Paper 1, questions will assess your geographical skills.

Memory jogger for Paper 2!

- My case study of a major city in an advanced country was of _____ .
- My case study of a major city in an emerging and developing country was of _____ .
- My case study of a low-income developing country was of _____ .
- My case study of attempts to achieve food security in one country was of _____ .
- My human fieldwork was on _____ (name of topic) and we collected data on _____ at (name of place) _____ .

Component 3 Geographical Exploration

This is assessed by Paper 3. There is no particular content for this component, but instead it draws on a range of topics and themes within Components 1 and 2.

- The exam questions will ask you to apply what you have learned to an unseen country, based on information in a Resource Booklet.

All three exam papers are quite different from each other.

Format of Paper 1

- **Time:** 1 hour 15 minutes.
- **Worth:** 70 marks in total – 52 on the four topics you've learned and 15 for physical geography fieldwork. An additional 3 marks are available for spelling, punctuation, grammar and use of specialist geographical terminology (SPaG), which is assessed on the 8-mark fieldwork question in Section B.
- **Counts for:** 35% of your final grade.
- **Number of sections:** two, assessing the topics described for Component 1 (see page 5).
- **All questions** are compulsory.

You must answer **all** questions as follows:

- **Section A** – with questions on each of four topics (Global Hazards, Changing Climate, Distinctive Landscapes and Sustaining Ecosystems), each worth 13 marks (52 marks in total).
- **Section B** – with questions on physical geography fieldwork. This section has 15 marks in total, plus 3 for SPaG, which is added to one 8-mark question.

Any resources you need to answer the questions are contained in a separate booklet.

Format of Paper 2

- **Time:** 1 hour 15 minutes.
- **Worth:** 70 marks in total – 52 on the four topics you have learned and 15 for physical geography fieldwork. An additional 3 marks are available for spelling, punctuation, grammar and use of specialist geographical terminology (SPaG), which is assessed on the 8-mark fieldwork question in Section B.
- **Counts for:** 35% of your final grade.
- **Number of sections:** two, assessing the topics described in Component 2 (see page 5).
- **All questions** are compulsory.

You must answer **all** questions as follows:

- Section A – with questions on each of four topics (Urban Futures, Dynamic Development, UK in the 21st Century and Resource Reliance), each worth 13 marks (52 marks in total).
- Section B – with questions on human geography fieldwork. This section has 15 marks in total, plus 3 for SPaG, which is added to one 8-mark question.

Any resources you need to answer the questions are contained in a separate booklet.

Format of Paper 3

- **Time:** 1 hour 30 minutes.
- **Worth:** 60 marks in total – 57 for geographical questions. An additional 3 marks are available for spelling, punctuation, grammar and use of specialist geographical terminology (SPaG), which are assessed in the final decision-making exercise.
- **Counts for:** 30% of your final grade.
- **Number of sections:** one.
- **All questions** are compulsory.

Paper 3 has a separate Resource Booklet. It consists of resources that will be needed for the questions set.

Question style

In each topic on each exam, the first questions are short, each worth between 1 and 4 marks.

- These involve a mix of multiple-choice, short answers or calculations.
- There are resource materials (data, photos, cartoons, etc.) on which you will be asked questions. These could include statistical skills, so remember you can use a calculator in each exam.
- You'll be expected to know what these resources are getting at from what you have learned.
- Detailed case study knowledge is only needed on particular case studies in Papers 1 and 2, though you can get marks for using examples.

All these questions are **point-marked** (see pages 14–15).

Later in each topic, questions require extended writing and are worth 6 or 8 marks. You need to have learned examples and case studies to answer these questions. Paper 3 also contains two questions worth 12 marks. Extended answers like these are marked using **levels** – from Level 1 (lowest) to Level 3 (highest) (see pages 10–13). These questions are likely to be on those parts where you have been taught examples (e.g. on Paper 1 a tectonic hazard and a tropical cyclone event, or on Paper 2 a low-income developing country).

One of the 8-mark questions on each of Papers 1 and 2 is also assessed for SPaG for 3 marks, making it worth 11 marks in total. The same is true for one of the 12-mark questions on Paper 3, making it worth 15 marks in total.

Answering the questions

Answering questions properly is the key to success. When you first read an exam question, check out the **command word** – that is, the word that the examiner uses to tell you what to do. The table below gives you the command words you can expect and the number of marks you can expect for each command word.

Command words

Command word	Typical number of marks	What it means	Example question
Identify/State/Name/Give	1	Find (e.g. on a photo) or give a simple word or statement	Identify the landform shown in the photo.
Define	1	Give a clear meaning	Define the term 'fertility rate'.
Calculate	1 or 2	Work out	Calculate the mean depth of the river in Figure 2.
Label	1 or 2	Print the name of, or write, on a map or diagram	Label features A and B of the cliff in Figure 4.
Draw	2 or 3	As in sketch or draw a line	Draw a line to complete the graph.
Compare	3	Identify similarities or differences	*(referring to a graph)* Compare the rate of population growth in cities x and y.
Describe	2, 3 or 4	Say what something is like; identify trends	Describe the features on the photo.
Suggest	2, 3 or 4	*(in an unfamiliar photo or graph)* Explain how or why something might occur	Suggest reasons for the increase shown in the graph.
Explain	2, 3, 4 or 6	Give reasons why something happens	Explain the rapid growth of one named mega-city.
Discuss	6, 8 or 12	Give an overview of a topic where there are different viewpoints	Discuss the ways in which climate change could be managed.
Examine	6, 8 or 12	Give reasons for something and judge which reason is more important	Examine reasons for the growth of one named LIDC city.
Assess	6, 8 or 12	Weigh up which is most or least important	Assess the need for coastal management.
Evaluate	6, 8 or 12	Make judgements about which is most or least effective	Evaluate the methods used in collecting data in your fieldwork.
To what extent / How far do you agree...?	6, 8 or 12	Show how far you agree or disagree with a statement	How far do mega-cities offer a better lifestyle for migrants than rural areas they have left?
Justify	12	Give reasons why you support a particular decision or opinion	*(in Paper 3)* Justify reasons for your choice.

Examiners have clear guidance about how to mark. They must mark fairly so that the first candidate's exam paper is marked in exactly the same way as the last candidate's.

You will be rewarded for what you know and can do. You won't lose marks for what you leave out. If your answer matches the best qualities in the mark scheme, then you'll get full marks.

Any questions that carry between 1 and 4 marks are **point marked** (that is, one mark for each correct point made) (see pages 14–15) and those that carry 6 marks or more are **level marked** (see pages 10–13). Be clear about what this means.

Understanding Assessment Objectives

Assessment Objectives (called AOs) are the things that examiners look for in marking your answers. There are four in GCSE Geography:

- AO1 – Knowledge recall
- AO2 – Understanding concepts, places and environments
- AO3 – Applying what you have learned to situations and making informed judgements
- AO4 – Geographical skills, which also includes fieldwork, statistics and maths skills.

Examples of the command words used for each AO and typical questions that could be set are shown in the table below.

Command word	Usual AO	Example of a question assessing this AO
Identify/State/Name/Give	AO1	Identify the landform shown in the photo.
Define	AO1	Define the term 'GDP'.
Calculate	AO4	Calculate the mean depth of the river shown in Figure 2.
Label	AO1	Label features A and B of the cliff in Figure 4.
Draw	AO4	Draw a line to complete the graph in Figure 3.
Compare	AO3	Compare the rate of population growth in cities x and y.
Describe	AO1 and AO2	Describe the features of a river meander.
Explain	AO1 and AO2	Explain the rapid growth of one mega-city you have studied.
Suggest	AO3	Suggest reasons for the increase shown in the graph.
Any 6 or 8 mark question	A mix of AO1, AO2 and AO3	Assess the impacts of a named tropical cyclone. Evaluate whether tectonic hazards have greater impacts on developed rather than on developing countries.
Justify (12 marks)	AO2 and AO3 (6 marks each)	(*in Paper 3, last question*) Justify the reasons for your choice.

Understanding the most demanding questions

The most demanding command words are tinted green in the table on page 9. As well as assessing AO1 and AO2, they assess AO3 and carry high marks.

The table shows that longer questions often combine marks for AO3 with marks for other AOs. Look at this example of where AO3 is used with AO2:

> Assess the impacts of a named tropical cyclone. **(8 marks)**

This involves knowing and understanding impacts of tropical cyclones (AO2 understanding) for 4 marks and then assessing how serious each impact is (AO3) for another 4 marks.

Sometimes AO3 is the only AO being assessed in a question. This is usually the case with fieldwork. Look at this example:

> Evaluate the methods used in collecting data in your fieldwork.
> **(8 marks)**

This involves applying your experience of fieldwork skills and making a judgement about how well or how accurately these worked (AO3).

In Paper 3, two AOs are assessed in the final 12-mark question:

> Justify the reasons for your choice. **(12 marks)**

This involves applying what you have learned (AO2) to what you read in the Resource Booklet (AO3) and then how well you make a judgement about which is the best option (AO3).

Level-marked questions

Questions worth 6, 8 or 12 marks are marked using levelled mark schemes. Examiners mark answers based on these.

- There are three levels for 6- and 8-mark questions. Level 1 is the lowest and Level 3 the highest (see the table below).
- There are four levels for 12-mark questions (see more detail on page 63).
- Note that it is not so much the number of points you make but the ways in which you explain and extend the points that matters.

Level	Marks	Description
3	7–8	• Explains very clearly • Makes detailed points, using extended explanations • Detailed examples of places and impacts are used • Well written, with full use of geographical terms • Makes detailed judgements based on evidence when asked to assess or evaluate
2	4–6	• Some fairly clear explanation • Two or three points are explained briefly • Examples are used, but vary in detail; places (e.g. countries) and impacts are named • Writes clearly, using some geographical terms • Makes some judgement when asked to assess or evaluate
1	1–3	• Limited or no explanation • One or two points are simply described but not developed • Most of the answer lacks detail or named examples • Places are poorly located (e.g. 'in Africa') • Few geographical terms or phrases are used • Makes no judgement when asked to assess or evaluate
	0	Nothing of credit

Answering demanding command words

The table below shows a detailed level-based mark scheme, which is used for all 6- and 8-mark questions. These assess a mix of AO1, AO2 and AO3.

- When they mark these questions, examiners do not mark points, but instead read the answer as a whole and judge it against the qualities shown in the table. They are looking for ways in which the answer is developed and explained.
- For 6 marks, you need to include two fully developed points. For 8 marks, you need about three extended and exemplified points.
- Level 3 is reserved for candidates who make judgements (e.g. assessing, showing the extent to which they agree), as the command word tells them to do. Candidates who just *explain* the impacts can only get Level 1 or 2. (The exception is in Paper 3, where four levels are used to assess the two 12-mark questions. See pages 61–65 for more detail.)

Study the mark scheme and then look at the sample answer on page 12, which is worth the full 8 marks. (You can find more detailed guidance on answering 6-, 8- and 12-mark questions on pages 23–65.)

Level	Marks	Description
3	**6-mark questions** 5–6 marks **8-mark questions** 6–8 marks	• Detailed knowledge (AO1) • Thorough understanding of the topic (AO2) • Information is relevant and detailed (AO2) • Thorough analysis of the question title (AO3) • Ideas are well developed with clear evidence (AO3) • Well-developed lines of reasoning (AO3) • Clear and logically structured argument (AO3)
2	**6-mark questions** 3–4 marks **8-mark questions** 3–5 marks	• Reasonable knowledge (AO1) • Reasonable understanding of the topic (AO2) • Information is generally relevant with some detail (AO2) • Some analysis of the question title (AO3) • Ideas are developed with some evidence (AO3) • Some lines of reasoning are present (AO3) • Argument is presented with some structure (AO3)
1	**6- and 8-mark questions** 1–2 marks	• Basic knowledge (AO1) • Basic understanding of the topic (AO2) • Information is often irrelevant or with little detail (AO2) • Little or no analysis of the question title (AO3) • No development of ideas, with limited evidence (AO3) • Unclear lines of reasoning (AO3) • Argument is basic with little structure (AO3)
	0 marks	• Nothing of credit

What makes a good Level 3 answer?

Read the 8-mark question and answer below.

> Assess the economic effects of a named tropical storm.

The storm is named. Always do this – you could limit yourself to Level 1 or 2 if you don't. The name doesn't get a mark but makes it possible to get the maximum mark. Notice the phrase 'most serious' – evidence that the candidate is assessing impact.

'Stormy winds and floods' introduce the first economic effects. Credit is given for the detailed explanation of economic effects – 'damaged buildings', 'which cost insurance companies and governments millions'. These are linked by the connective phrase 'which cost'. This turns a Level 1 or Level 2 point about 'damaging buildings' into Level 3 by adding detail. The candidate assesses the storm as the 'worst known'.

In Cyclone Aila, which affected Bangladesh in 2009, the economic effects were enormous and most serious among the poor. The cyclone brought some of the worst known stormy winds and floods. This damaged buildings, which cost insurance companies and governments millions. More storms also caused erosion of flood defences, which flooded villages and farmland, costing huge amounts to replace and repair, and destroyed crops. For many farmers and families, this meant loss of homes and crops, making their poverty worse and forcing some to leave the land and move to Dhaka, the capital, for work.

'Erosion of flood defences' is also an economic impact. It is extended with 'flooded villages and farmland' and 'costing huge amounts to replace and repair'. The phrase 'costing huge amounts' is a judgement of its seriousness, making this answer Level 3 and showing that the candidate is assessing.

'loss of homes and crops' is evidence of another economic impact. The candidate assesses the seriousness of loss of crops – it makes poverty worse and forces people to leave the land, so answering the command word 'Assess'.

Make sure you answer the question set. Good answers are often shorter and more focused – longer answers can stray off the point. To help you focus, unpick the question, as follows.

> Using examples, explain how coastal erosion can create different landforms along a coast.
>
> **(8 marks)**

You must give examples such as landforms (e.g. arch, stack) or places where they occur.

The focus – coastal erosion. You need to explain processes (e.g. hydraulic action) and how they lead to landforms (e.g. caves).

You must name at least three specific landforms.

This question is about explaining processes that lead to different landforms. It's important that you explain why these processes happen – don't just describe. Good explanation takes you to Level 3.

Using case studies

Candidates often worry about how to learn or write a good case study. The following question requires the use of examples.

Assess the success of regeneration in one named UK city. **(8 marks)**

A good example to use for this question is Birmingham (see Student Book sections 5.8–5.12). Use other examples of regeneration schemes if you have studied them. Plan your case studies using a spider diagram, as below, to organise your thoughts.

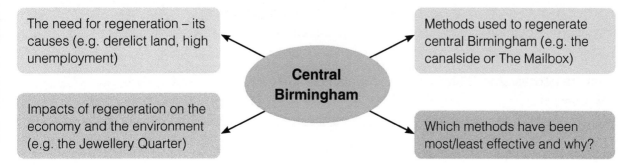

From a spider diagram, you can build up more detailed notes, such as:

- The need for regeneration – draw two 'legs' to explain economic causes (e.g. lack of jobs) and environmental causes (e.g. derelict land).
- Methods used to regenerate central Birmingham – draw three 'legs' to explain the methods used to provide housing, build the economy and improve the environment.
- Impacts of regeneration on the economy and the environment – you could sub-divide these too, into economic, social and environmental impacts.
- Finally, you could draw two 'legs' to show which methods have been effective and which have not.

On your marks

Maximising marks on shorter questions

- **In this section you'll learn how to maximise marks on questions worth 1–4 marks.**

Understanding point marking

Answering questions properly is the key to success. Check two things:

- the **command word** – this is what the examiner wants you to do (see page 8)
- the **number of marks** – this tells you how many points to make.

Questions carrying up to 4 marks are point marked – that means you get a mark for every correct point you make. Look at this question:

> Rainforests are ecosystems. State **one** way in which people can protect ecosystems. **(1 mark)**

One mark means you need to name one way of protecting ecosystems, e.g.

- set up a national park
- make it illegal to carry out logging.

The mark scheme tells examiners which points they can mark as correct.

Extending an answer – 'Describe'

Success on longer questions with more marks means knowing how to turn 1 mark into 2, or 2 into 3 marks. To achieve this, you need to **develop** answers. Look at this question:

> Rainforests are ecosystems. Describe **one** way in which humans can protect ecosystems. **(2 marks)**

This time, it is not enough to name one way of protecting an ecosystem. To earn 2 marks, you must do one of the following:

- **Extend the point** by describing it in more detail, e.g.
  Make it illegal to carry out logging where forest habitats are protected for animals.
- **Give an example** of what you are describing, e.g.
  Make it illegal to carry out logging, for example like the rainforests in large areas of Brazil.
- **Give a reason** why something occurs, e.g.
  Make it illegal to carry out logging because that is the biggest danger to rainforest ecosystems.

Extending an answer – 'Explain'

Now consider this question:

> Explain one possible economic impact of climate change.   **(2 marks)**

This question asks you to 'explain' (give reasons for) the impacts. That means you shouldn't just state what the impact is but must say **why** it occurs. In the following examples, a tick (√) shows where a mark is earned.

> Rising sea level might mean farmland near the coast gets flooded ✔

This is an impact but is only worth 1 mark as it simply says one thing.

However, the following answer is worth 2 marks:

> Rising sea level might mean farmland near the coast gets flooded ✔ so that farmers lose their crops ✔

'So' is one of the most useful words you'll ever learn to help you get higher marks. Other useful connecting words/phrases include 'therefore' and 'which leads to'.

The explanation has been **extended** to make it worth a second mark.

Other examples of extended answers include:

> Sea level change might mean farmland near the coast gets flooded ✔ and farmers would lose crops, e.g. rice ✔

This is an economic impact, extended with an **example**, so it gains a second mark.

> Sea level change means farmers near the coast might lose rice crops ✔ if saltwater flooded the fields as rice is a freshwater plant ✔

This answer has been **explained**, giving a reason why crops are lost.

Lines of reasoning

Sometimes a question will ask you to give a full explanation for 4 marks. In the following example, you have to think of four points that run in a sequence to explain the process of how one thing leads to another.

> Explain how volcanoes may form along a constructive plate margin.
> **(4 marks)**

Below is an example of a **line of reasoning** – an explanation of a process, e.g. 'X happens, which leads to y and then to z'.

> As the plates pull apart ✔, a plume of magma rises to the surface to fill the gap ✔. On constructive plate margins, this is often basaltic lava, which flows easily away from the boundary before it solidifies ✔. More lava creates another layer on top of the first layer ✔.

On your marks

Nailing the 4-mark questions

- **In this section you'll learn how to maximise marks on 4-mark questions.**

The question below is worth 4 marks and is points marked.

Use the BUG example on page 17 to plan your own answer.

Question

Study **Fig. 1**, a photo showing a house damaged by Cyclone Haiyan in a rural area of the Philippines in 2013.

Fig. 1

Using **Fig. 1** and your own knowledge, explain two reasons why tropical cyclones have such a big impact in developing countries like the Philippines.

(4 marks)

1 Plan your answer

Before attempting to answer the question, remember to **BUG** it. That means:

✓ **Box** the command word.
✓ **Underline** the following:
  - the theme
  - the focus
  - any evidence required
  - the number of examples needed.
✓ **Glance** back over the question to make sure you include everything in your answer.

Use the BUG example on page 17 to plan your own answer.

Five steps to help you write top quality answers

The following five steps are used in this section to help you get the best marks.

1 **Plan your answer** – decide what to include and how to structure your answer.

2 **Write your answer** – use the answer spaces to complete your answer.

3 **Mark your answer** – use the mark scheme to self- or peer-mark your answer. You can also use this to assess sample answers in step 4 below.

4 **Sample answers** – sample answers show you how to maximise marks for a question.

5 **Marked sample answers** – these are the same answers as for step 4, but are marked and annotated so that you can compare them with your own answers.

Evidence: Support your answer with information from the photo **and** from your own knowledge. You must do both to get 4 marks.

Command word: Give reasons why something happens.

Using **Fig. 1** and your own knowledge, explain two reasons why tropical cyclones have such a big impact on developing countries like the Philippines. **(4 marks)**

Theme: This question is linked to the theme of tropical storms, assessed in Paper 1, Section A of your exam. The question is compulsory.

Focus: You must consider why the hazard has such an impact, not just describe what you see in the photo.

Focus and number of examples: The question asks for two specific reasons about developing countries, so you must offer two **and** expand them with more detail.

PEEL your answer

Use PEEL notes to structure your answer. This will help you to communicate your ideas to the examiner in the clearest way. PEEL has four stages.

- **P**oint – make two points for this question. Use sentences, not bullet points.
- **E**xplain – give reasons for each point. Use sentence starters such as: 'This is because ...', 'One reason is ...'.
- **E**vidence – include facts and other details from named examples or from the photo to support each point.
- **L**ink – link the two points to each other, using PEE sentence starters such as: 'A second way is ...' or 'Secondly ...'. You'll learn more about how to do this on 6- and 8-mark questions (see pages 24, 32, 40 and 48).

Tip

For all questions using 'Explain' as a command word, you will be marked on the number of points you make. For 4 marks, that means two developed points.

2 Write your answer

Using **Fig. 1** and your own knowledge, explain two reasons why tropical cyclones have such a big impact in developing countries like the Philippines. **(4 marks)**

1._____

_____

2._____

_____

3 Mark your answer

1. To help you to identify well-structured points in the answer, highlight the:

- points in red
- explanations in orange
- evidence in blue.

2. Use the mark scheme below to decide what mark to give.

Mark scheme

The candidate must refer to the photo **and** to their own knowledge. Two points from the photo are acceptable if reasons clearly come from the candidate's own knowledge. Accept any of the following points for one mark each, with development as shown in italics:

- The photo shows a collapsed house (√), *which has probably been caused by weak building regulations* (√)
- Poor quality housing (√) *has not been able to withstand the strong winds of a tropical cyclone* (√)
- People in rural areas like in the photo may be vulnerable (√) *because they are isolated* (√)
- Building materials, e.g. wood, bamboo (√), *show the building was probably cheap to build but weak* (√)
- Plus any other relevant points on merit

4 Sample answer

Read through these two sample answers. Go through each one using the three colours in step 3 above and decide how many marks each is worth.

Sample answer 1

1. Tropical cyclones have such a big impact in countries like this because houses like the one in the photo would have collapsed because of the high winds in a tropical cyclone.

2. Tropical cyclones affect the poor most of all as they have no resilience because they have no savings to fall back on if they lose their house.

Strengths of the answer			
Ways to improve the answer			
Level		Mark	

Sample answer 2

1. Wooden shacks like the one in the photo are not strong enough to stand up to strong hurricane winds.

2. People in poor countries often live in houses like this on land that isn't theirs.

Strengths of the answer			
Ways to improve the answer			
Level		Mark	

5 Marked sample answers

The sample answers are marked below. The text has been highlighted as follows to show how well each answer has structured points:

- points in red

- explanations in orange

- evidence in blue.

A tick (√) is shown for each mark the candidate earns.

? Question recap

Using **Fig. 1** and your own knowledge, explain two reasons why tropical cyclones have such a big impact in developing countries like the Philippines.

Marked sample answer 1

1. Tropical cyclones have such a big impact in countries like this because houses would like the one in the photo would have collapsed ✔ because of the high winds in a tropical cyclone ✔ .

2. Tropical cyclones affect the poor most of all as they have no resilience ✔ because they have no savings to fall back on if they lose their house ✔ .

Evidence – collapsed wooden building in the photo

Explanation – suggests that high winds destroyed it

Point – the poor suffer greatest impact because of lack of resilience

Explanation – suggests that the poor have no savings

✓ Examiner feedback

The candidate uses the photo to identify features that help to answer the question in the first point and their own knowledge about the impacts of tropical cyclones on poorer people in the second point. Each point is then extended, so that the answer earns all 4 marks.

Marked sample answer 2

1. Wooden shacks like the one in the photo would not be strong enough to stand up to strong hurricane winds.

2. People in poor countries often live in houses like this on land that isn't theirs.

Evidence – specific building materials from the photo

Explanation – gives a reason why houses are not strong

✓ Examiner feedback

This candidate refers to the photo to identify features about building materials and then how these cannot resist strong hurricane winds. However, although in the second point the candidate gives reasons why poor people are more vulnerable, it doesn't answer this question. The answer therefore earns just 2 marks.

Now try this one!

Follow the stages from the previous example to tackle a different 4-mark question.

Question

Study **Fig. 2**

Country	HDI	Death rate per 1000 population	% population with access to safe water
Japan	0.891	9.51	100
Brazil	0.755	6.58	98
Zimbabwe	0.509	10.13	77

Fig. 2 – *A table showing three indicators of development for three countries*

Explain the strengths and limitations of **one** of the indicators in **Fig. 2** in seeking to understand a country's level of development.   **(4 marks)**

1 Plan your answer

Before attempting to answer the question, remember to **BUG** it. Use the guidelines on page 16. Annotate it in the margin.

> Explain the strengths and limitations of **one** of the indicators in **Fig. 2** in seeking to understand a country's level of development.   **(4 marks)**

PEEL your answer

Use PEEL notes to structure your answer. Use the guidelines on page 17.

2 Write your answer

> Explain the strengths and limitations of **one** of the indicators in **Fig. 2** in seeking to understand a country's level of development.   **(4 marks)**

_____

_____

_____

_____

_____

_____

_____

_____

3 Mark your answer

1. To help you to identify well-structured points in the answer, highlight the:

   • points in red   • explanations in orange   • evidence in blue.

2. Use the mark scheme below to decide what mark to give.

Mark scheme

Award marks as follows: candidates must explain both a strength and a limitation for their chosen indicator in Fig. 2. Possible strengths and weaknesses include:

Indicator	Strengths	Weaknesses
HDI	• Uses a range of indicators (√), giving a more accurate picture (√) • Shows how much people benefit (√) from increased GDP (√)	• May not reflect high GDP (√) if wealth is not shared (√)
Death rate per 1000 population	• A low figure indicates wealth (√) because it shows people have good health (√)	• May not increase with GDP (√) because a country might not improve health services (√)
% population with access to safe water	• Water quality improves from higher spending (√) as a country becomes affluent (√)	• Some countries like Nigeria do not have high % of safe water (√) because wealth goes to a few and not people as a whole (√)

---

4 Sample answer

Read through this sample answer. Go through it using the three colours in step 3 above and decide how many marks it is worth.

? Question recap

Explain the strengths and limitations of any **one** of the indicators in **Fig. 2** in seeking to understand a country's level of development.

Sample answer 3

HDI is a good measure of a country's development because it shows how well developed a country is socially as well as economically. It is a single figure, which combines GDP (to show how wealthy a country is) with literacy (which shows the level of education) and infant mortality (which shows the level of healthcare). So it is a good way of showing how much money is spent on health and education. HDI has a disadvantage because wealthy countries might not have a high HDI figure if wealth is concentrated in the hands of a few wealthy people (like Saudi Arabia), and so does not get spent on people.

Strengths of the answer	
Ways to improve the answer	
Level		**Mark**	

⑤ Marked sample answer

Sample answer 3 is marked below. The text is highlighted as follows:

- points in red

- explanations in orange

- evidence in blue.

 Question recap

Explain the strengths and limitations of any **one** of the indicators in **Fig. 2** in seeking to understand a country's level of development.

Marked sample answer 3

Point – immediately makes a judgement that helps to answer the question

Explanation – explains how HDI is useful socially and economically

Evidence – a really clear statement showing the evidence to support the candidate's judgement about HDI

HDI is a good measure of a country's development because it shows how well developed a country is socially as well as economically. It is a single figure, which combines GDP (to show how wealthy a country is) with literacy (which shows the level of education) and infant mortality (which shows the level of healthcare). So it is a good way of showing how much money is spent on health and education. HDI has a disadvantage because wealthy countries might not have a high HDI figure if wealth is concentrated in the hands of a few wealthy people (like Saudi Arabia), and so does not get spent on people.

Point – makes a judgement about health and education

Point – only a basic point but it helps to balance the answer with a disadvantage as well as an advantage

Explanation – an explanation of the point made

 Examiner feedback

The candidate knows what HDI is and how it is measured, and can also explain its advantage in combining three measures. Two advantages show how HDI is calculated and a disadvantage shows why it does not work in countries like Saudi Arabia. The candidate refers to evidence to support the points made. The answer therefore earns all 4 marks.

- **In this section you'll learn how to tackle 6- and 8-mark questions that use 'Discuss' as a command word.**

Six- and eight-mark questions – what's different?

By now, you should have got the hang of answering 4-mark questions. Six- and eight-mark questions differ from 4-mark questions because they are marked using **levels**, not points. They are marked using three levels, where Level 3 is the most challenging. Level 3 is worth 5–6 marks (on 6-mark questions) or 7–8 marks (on 8-mark questions).

Level 3 means writing to a higher standard.

- Tougher command words are used. 'Describe', 'Explain' and 'Suggest' tend to be used in 4-mark questions. 'Discuss', 'Assess', 'Evaluate' and 'Examine' tend to be used in 6- and 8-mark questions.
- You need to develop an argument in your answer. You could be asked how far you agree with a statement or to what extent do you think something occurs (like the example below).

A **4-mark question** might ask:

'Explain two impacts of a volcanic eruption on climate.'

A **6- or 8-mark question** might ask:

'To what extent can volcanic eruptions cause important changes to the global climate?'

Question

Study **Fig. 1**, a photo showing a rainforest in Borneo, Indonesia that has been cleared to make way for a plantation. The land is now used as a plantation for farming.

Fig. 1

Using **Fig. 1** and your own knowledge, discuss the impacts of rainforest clearance.

(6 marks)

Five steps to help you write top quality answers

The following five steps are used in this section to help you get the best marks.

1

Plan your answer – decide what to include and how to structure your answer.

2

Write your answer – use the answer spaces to complete your answer.

3

Mark your answer – use the mark scheme to self- or peer-mark your answer. You can also use this to assess sample answers in step 4 below.

4

Sample answers – sample answers show you how to maximise marks for a question.

5

Marked sample answers – these are the same answers as for step 4, but are marked and annotated so that you can compare them with your own answers.

1 Plan your answer

Before attempting to answer the question, remember to **BUG** it.
That means:

✓ **Box** the command word.
✓ **Underline** the following:
  - the theme
  - the focus
  - any evidence required
  - the number of examples needed.
✓ **Glance** back over the question to make sure you include everything in your answer.

Use the BUG example below to plan your own answer.

Remember!

The command word 'Discuss' assesses AO2 (your knowledge and understanding of the topic) and AO3 (your ability to apply what you know and understand to the question).

Evidence: Support your answer with information from the photo **and** from your own knowledge. You must do both to get top marks.

Command word: Give an overview of a topic where there are different viewpoints. As well as explaining impacts, you need to decide whether these are positive or negative.

Using Fig. 1 and your own knowledge, discuss the impacts of rainforest clearance.

(6 marks)

Theme: This question is linked to Topic 4, Sustaining Ecosystems, assessed in Paper 1, Section A of your exam. The question is compulsory.

Focus: You must explain reasons why rainforest clearance can have such impacts, based on what you've studied, as well as what's in the photo.

Focus and number of examples: The focus is impacts – i.e. things affected by forest clearance. 6-and 8-mark questions don't state how many impacts – but you probably need to explain and develop two for a 6-mark question and three for a 8-mark question, written in paragraphs.

PEEL your answer

Use PEEL notes to structure your answer. This will help you to communicate your ideas to the examiner in the clearest way. PEEL has four stages.

- **P**oint – give three impacts for this question. Use sentences, not bullet points.
- **E**xplain – give reasons for each point. Use sentence starters such as: 'This is because ...', 'One reason is ...'.
- **E**vidence – include facts and other details from named examples or from the photo to support each point.
- **L**ink – link back to the question, using PEE sentence starters such as: 'This shows how ...' or 'The impacts are therefore greatest when rainforests are ...'. Finish with a one-sentence conclusion.

Planning grid

Use this planning grid to help you write high-quality paragraphs. Remember to include links to show how your points relate to each other and to the question.

 **?** **Question recap**

Using **Fig. 1** and your own knowledge, discuss the impacts of rainforest clearance.

	PEE Paragraph 1	PEE Paragraph 2
Point		
Explanation		
Evidence *(from the photo or your own knowledge)*		
Link – a mini-conclusion		

2 Write your answer

Using **Fig. 1** and your own knowledge, discuss the impacts of rainforest clearance.

(6 marks)

_____

_____

_____

_____

_____

_____

_____

_____

_____

_____

_____

_____

_____

_____

_____

_____

_____

Tip

'Discuss' means using a range of examples

Don't just describe and explain. If the question asks you to 'Discuss', it wants you to cover a range of impacts.

For example, 'Discuss the impacts of rainforest clearance' wants you to say whether impacts are positive or negative, or perhaps whether they are economic, social or environmental.

One way of doing this is in a **mini-conclusion** – it need only be a sentence or two.

Remember!

'Discuss' assesses AO2 (knowledge and understanding) and AO3 (application).

Strengths of the answer	
Ways to improve the answer	
Level	**Mark**	

3 Mark your answer

1. To help you to identify well-structured points in the answer, highlight the:

- points in red

- explanations in orange

- evidence in blue.

Question recap

Using **Fig. 1** and your own knowledge, discuss the impacts of rainforest clearance.

2. Use the mark scheme below to decide what mark to give. Six-mark questions are not marked using individual points, but instead you should choose a level and a mark based upon the quality of the answer as a whole.

Level	Marks	Description	Examples
3 (Well-developed / Thorough)	5–6	**For AO2** • Thorough understanding of the topic • Information is relevant and detailed **For AO3** • Thorough analysis of the question title • Ideas are well developed, with clear evidence • Well-developed lines of reasoning • Clear and logically structured argument	• *The removal of forest cover would expose the soils to heavy tropical rains, which would erode them, making the land useless for farming.* • *The bare soil in the photo shows how exposed it would be to erosion by rain and surface runoff.*
2 (Developed / Reasonable)	3–4	**For AO2** • Reasonable understanding of the topic • Information is generally relevant with some detail **For AO3** • Some analysis of the question title • Ideas are developed, with some evidence • Some lines of reasoning are present • Argument is presented with some structure	• *Removing the trees would mean less protection for the soil from heavy rain – runoff would occur and probably take the soil with it.* • *The photo shows little vegetation to protect the soil so it would probably be lost.*
1 (Simple/ Basic)	1–2	**For AO2** • Basic understanding of the topic • Information is often irrelevant or in little detail **For AO3** • Little or no analysis of the question title • No development of ideas; limited evidence • Unclear lines of reasoning • Argument is basic with little structure	• *The land is all bare and there are no trees there. The rain would wash it away.* • *The photo shows all the trees have been cut and burned and there's nothing there.*
	0	No accurate response	

4 Sample answers

Read the two sample answers below. Go through each one using the three colours in step 3. Use the level descriptions to decide how many marks each answer is worth, assessing AO2 (knowledge and understanding) and AO3 (application).

Question recap

Using **Fig. 1** and your own knowledge, discuss the impacts of rainforest clearance.

Sample answer 4

The forest looks like it has been cleared by burning. The land looks full of tree roots, meaning that it will not be easy to plant crops. The soil is black, which is probably ash from all the burnt trees after the fires have gone out. The next time it rains, the ash will probably get washed away because it looks like the land is sloping a bit, and farmers might find there is no soil left by the time they get to plant their crops. There is no wildlife, which probably got killed in the fires. Lots of rainforests get cleared by burning like this.

Strengths of the answer			
Ways to improve the answer			
Level		**Mark**	

Sample answer 5

Clearing rainforest areas like this can be disastrous. The forest cover has been cleared and burned. It used to shelter the soil so that when it rained heavily the rain would be intercepted and would drip slowly into the soil. Now, if there's a storm, the rain will run off and will probably take the soil with it because there's nothing to protect it.

Soils in rainforests are infertile, so that clearing land for plantations may not be a good idea anyway. Probably the ash that's in the photo would be the only fertile part of the soil. So clearing forests is not likely to have any benefits for farmers.

Strengths of the answer			
Ways to improve the answer			
Level		**Mark**	

5 Marked sample answers

The sample answers are marked below. The text has been highlighted to show how well each answer has structured points:

- points in red   • explanations in orange   • evidence in blue
- judgements are underlined. These are important for reaching Level 3 on questions using the command word 'Discuss'.

Marked sample answer 4

Evidence – evidence from the photo but not linked to impacts of clearing rainforest

Evidence – more evidence from the photo but, again, not about impacts

> The forest looks like it has been cleared by burning. The land looks full of tree roots, meaning that it will not be easy to plant crops. The soil is black, which is probably ash from all the burnt trees after the fires have gone out. The next time it rains, the ash will probably get washed away because it looks like the land is sloping a bit, and farmers might find there is no soil left by the time they get to plant their crops. There is no wildlife, which probably got killed in the fires. Lots of rainforests get cleared by burning like this.

Point – makes a point, describing an impact of clearing the forest

Explanation – explains one of the impacts of clearing forest, i.e. soil erosion

Explanation – this brief explanation does tackle one of the impacts of clearance

Evidence – a third observation from the photo though, again, not about impacts

 Examiner feedback

The descriptors for Level 2 just about apply to this answer as follows:

For AO2

- *'Reasonable understanding of the topic'* and *'Information is generally relevant with some detail'* – the candidate understands some impacts of rainforest clearance. This is general rather than detailed, e.g. there is little terminology (e.g. soil erosion).

For AO3

- *'Some analysis of the question title'* and *'Ideas are developed with some evidence'* – the two explanations show that the candidate is using evidence on the photo to suggest consequences of rainforest clearance.
- *'Some lines of reasoning are present'* and *'Argument is presented with some structure'* – the candidate develops an argument.

By partly meeting the descriptors, the answer is lower Level 2 and therefore earns 3 marks.

Marked sample answer 5

Judgement – makes a clear judgement at the start

Evidence – observes one impact from the photo

Explanation – explains what the forest would be like before clearance (essential to understanding impacts)

> Clearing rainforest areas like this can be disastrous. The forest cover has been cleared and burned. It used to shelter the soil so that when it rained heavily the rain would be intercepted and would drip slowly into the soil. Now, if there's a storm, the rain will run off and will probably take the soil with it because there's nothing to protect it.
>
> Soils in rainforests are infertile, so that clearing land for plantations may not be a good idea anyway. Probably the ash that's in the photo would be the only fertile part of the soil. So clearing forests is not likely to have any benefits for farmers.

Point – describes one impact (surface runoff)

Point – describes a second impact (soil erosion)

Explanation – explaind why erosion occurs

Point – makes a point to support the next judgement, which is clarified

Evidence – observes the ash and uses this to support the point about soils

Judgement – a third judgement about clearance

Judgement – makes a clear judgement about clearance

 Examiner feedback

The descriptors for Level 3 apply to this answer as follows:

For AO2

- *'Information is relevant and detailed'* with *'thorough understanding of the topic'* – the candidate understands the impacts about forest, rainfall runoff and soil erosion.

For AO3

- *'Ideas are well developed with clear evidence'* – the candidate uses evidence from the photo to support impacts.
- There are *'Well-developed lines of reasoning'* and *'Clear and logically structured argument'* – the candidate makes three supported, well-evidenced judgements.

By meeting these descriptors fully, the answer is top Level 3 and earns 6 marks.

- **In this section you'll learn how to tackle 6- and 8-mark questions that use 'Assess' as a command word.**

The following five steps are used in this section to help you get the best marks.

Question

Study **Fig. 1**, a photo showing deposition of sediment along a stretch of coast in South Australia.

Fig. 1

Using **Fig. 1** and your own knowledge, assess the part played by sediment deposition in creating coastal landscapes.

(8 marks + 3 marks for SPaG)

1. **Plan your answer** – decide what to include and how to structure your answer.

2. **Write your answer** – use the answer spaces to complete your answer.

3. **Mark your answer** – use the mark scheme to self- or peer-mark your answer. You can also use this to assess sample answers in step 4 below.

4. **Sample answers** – sample answers show you how to maximise marks for a question.

5. **Marked sample answers** – these are the same answers as for step 4, but are marked and annotated so that you can compare them with your own answers.

How is SPaG assessed?

One 8-mark question on each of Papers 1 and 2 will assess your accuracy of spelling, punctuation, grammar and the use of specialist terminology (known as SPaG). In each of these questions, three marks are allocated as follows:

- High performance – 3 marks
- Intermediate performance – 2 marks
- Threshold performance – 1 mark.

Examiners mark SPaG based on your:

- spelling accuracy, including capitalisation
- punctuation – the use of commas, full stops and semi-colons. If reading an answer aloud leaves you gasping for breath, it needs more punctuation
- syntax – the quality of your grammar
- paragraphing.

1 Plan your answer

Before attempting to answer the question, remember to **BUG** it.
That means:

✓ **Box** the command word.
✓ **Underline** the following:
  • the theme
  • the focus
  • any evidence required
  • the number of examples needed.
✓ **Glance** back over the question to make sure you include everything in your answer.

Annotate the question in the margin.

> Using **Fig. 1**, and your own knowledge assess the part played by sediment deposition in creating coastal landscapes.
>
> **(8 marks plus 3 marks SPaG)**

Remember!

The command word 'Assess' assesses AO2 (your understanding of a topic and recognising what you see in the photo) and AO3 (your ability to apply what you know and understand, and can see in the photo, to the question).

PEEL your answer

Use PEEL notes to structure your answer. This will help you to communicate your ideas to the examiner in the clearest way. PEEL has four stages.

• **P**oint – give at least three pieces of evidence for this question. Use sentences, not bullet points.
• **E**xplain – give reasons for each piece of evidence and how deposition creates coastal landscapes. Use sentence starters such as: 'This is because ...', 'One reason is ...'.
• **E**vidence – include details from the photo to support each piece of evidence.
• **L**ink – link back to the question about the part that sediment contributes to coastal landscapes, using PEE sentence starters. Finish with a one-sentence conclusion about the contribution that sediment deposition can make. Is it great or small?

 Tip

'Assess' means stating how strong the evidence is

If the question asks you to 'Assess', it wants you to show the strength of evidence.

For example, if a coastal spit is the most significant feature along a stretch of coast, then sediment deposition makes a big contribution.

Draw your argument together in a **mini-conclusion** – it need only be a sentence or two.

Planning grid

Use this planning grid to help you write high-quality paragraphs. Remember to include links to show how your points relate to each other and to the question. Note that this is an 8-mark question, so needs three PEE paragraphs.

Note that there is a fourth row to help you focus on the word 'Assess'. In this question, remember to **assess the evidence**.

Question recap

Using **Fig. 1** and your own knowledge, assess the part played by sediment deposition in creating coastal landscapes.

	PEE Paragraph 1	PEE Paragraph 2	PEE Paragraph 3
Point			
Explanation			
Evidence (from the photo and your own knowledge)			
Link back to the question – a mini-conclusion (assess the part played by sediment deposition)			

2 Write your answer

Using **Fig. 1** and your own knowledge, assess the part played by sediment deposition in creating coastal landscapes.

(8 marks + 3 marks for SPaG)

Remember!

'Assess' assesses AO2 (knowledge and understanding) and AO3 (application).

Strengths of the answer	
Ways to improve the answer	

Answer level		Mark out of 8	
SPaG level		Mark out of 3	

3 Mark your answer

1. To help you to identify well-structured points in the answer, highlight the:

   - points in red   • explanations in orange   • evidence in blue
   - underline any links to the question that show assessment of the part played by sediment deposition.

2. Use the mark scheme below to decide what mark to give. 8-mark questions are not marked using individual points, but instead you should choose a level and a mark based upon the quality of the answer as a whole.

Level	Marks	Description	Examples
3 (Well-developed / Thorough)	7–8	**For AO2** • Thorough understanding of the topic • Information is relevant and detailed **For AO3** • Thorough analysis of the question title • Ideas are well developed with clear evidence • Well-developed lines of reasoning • Clear and logically structured argument	• *The coastal spit shown has been formed by two processes. The main one is longshore drift, caused by winds creating waves that hit the shore at an angle.* • *Figure 3 shows a coastal spit that has forced the river to divert from where it used to reach the sea. This shows the impact of sediment – it can divert features such as rivers.* • *Spits are really significant landforms, like Spurn Head in East Yorkshire, which shelters the Humber from storms.*
2 (Developed / Reasonable)	4–6	**For AO2** • Reasonable understanding of the topic • Information is generally relevant with some detail **For AO3** • Some analysis of the question title • Ideas are developed with some evidence • Some lines of reasoning present • Argument is presented with some structure	• *Coastal spits are formed when waves break on the shore at an angle and take sediment along the coast, forming a long sandy headland into the water.* • *Figure 3 shows how the river stops the spit from forming a bar, which would join the two bits of coast together. So deposition can create important landforms.* • *There might be many coastal deposits along a coast, like sandy beaches, leading to resorts like Brighton.*
1 (Simple/ Basic)	1–3	**For AO2** • Basic understanding of the topic • Information is often irrelevant or in little detail **For AO3** • Little or no analysis of the question title • No development of ideas; limited evidence • Unclear lines of reasoning • Argument is basic with little structure	• *The spit comes from waves that break on the beach and longshore drift takes place.* • *The photo shows a sandy beach that reaches almost across the river.* • *Deposition creates many features like spits and beaches.*
	0	No accurate response	

Sample answer

Cover page 37 with a sheet of paper, so you are not tempted to look at it.

Read the sample answer below. Go through it using the three colours in step 3, including underlining any points that are assessing. Use the level descriptions to decide how many marks it is worth, assessing AO2 (knowledge and understanding) and AO3 (application). Remember to give a mark for SPaG.

 Question recap

Using **Fig. 1** and your own knowledge, assess the part played by sediment deposition in creating coastal landscapes.

Sample answer 6

The photo shows a spit of sand formed by deposition along the beach. The waves approach at an angle and swash takes the sand up the beach, where it runs back down in a zigzag pattern. Further waves repeat the process, so an elongated spit is formed. The spit in the photo moved until it reached the river and then the river current shaped it where it runs out to sea. The river in the photo has been diverted around the spit. Deposition can therefore divert river flow, showing how important it is.

Another depositional landform is a sand bar, which is like a spit except that there is no river to prevent movement of sand. The bar develops until it cuts off a lagoon. The lagoon can create important wildlife refuges because freshwater behind the bar remains sheltered and ideal for wild fowl, especially in winter. This means that deposition can create important features of coastal landscapes like mud flats behind a spit, which are areas of calm water away from storms.

The final contribution made by coastal deposition is beaches, which have physical impacts because they protect cliffs from erosion by absorbing friction from advancing waves. Where longshore drift moves beach material away, it may increase coastal retreat.

Strengths of the answer	
Ways to improve the answer	

Answer level		**Mark out of 8**	
SPaG level		**Mark out of 3**	

5 Marked sample answer

The sample answer on page 36 is marked below. The text has been highlighted to show how well it has structured points:

- points in red
- explanations in orange
- evidence in blue
- judgements are underlined. These are important for reaching Level 3 on questions using the command word 'Assess'.

Marked sample answer 6

The photo shows a spit formed of sand formed by deposition along the beach. The waves approach at an angle and swash takes the sand up the beach, where it runs back down in a zigzag pattern. Further waves repeat the process, so an elongated spit is formed. The spit in the photo moved until it reached the river and then the river current shaped it where it runs out to sea. The river in the photo has been diverted around the spit. Deposition can therefore divert river flow, showing how important it is.

Another depositional landform is a sand bar, which is like a spit except that there is no river to prevent movement of sand. The bar develops until it cuts off a lagoon. The lagoon can create important wildlife refuges because freshwater behind the bar remains sheltered and ideal for wild fowl, especially in winter. This means that deposition can create important features of coastal landscapes like mud flats behind a spit, which are areas of calm water away from storms.

The final contribution made by coastal deposition is beaches, which have physical impacts because they protect cliffs from erosion by absorbing friction from advancing waves. Where longshore drift moves beach material away, it may increase coastal retreat.

Point – identifies a spit and makes it clear it is depositional

Explanation – describes the process that forms spits

Evidence – evidences the process from the photo. This kind of evidence is important when you need to explain processes as a sequence of stages

Assesses the importance of depositional features, linking back to the question (here the link is assessing)

Point – identifies a sand bar and makes it clear it is depositional

Explanation – explains the process of bar formation

Assesses the importance of features of landscapes, using the question wording

Point – names a third depositional landform (beaches)

Explanation – explains the importance of beaches

Evidence – exemplifies, using mud flats as important features

Examiner feedback

This is a strong answer. The candidate explains three landforms (AO2), including using the photo to identify features. The photo is used well in the first paragraph, where the candidate shows some good explanation and some contribution made by sediment deposition (AO3). The answer needs a final mini-conclusion in the last sentence (AO3).

The descriptors for Level 3 apply to this answer as follows:

For AO2

- *'Thorough understanding of the topic'* and *'Information is relevant and detailed'* – the candidate describes landform formation in some detail. Landforms are identified and processes explained thoroughly.

For AO3

- *'Thorough analysis of the question title'* and *'Ideas are well developed with clear evidence* – the candidate makes assessments of how important sediment deposition is.
- There are *'Well-developed lines of reasoning* and a *'Clear and logically structured argument'.*
- *'Makes judgements supported by evidence'* – the candidate refers to the photo in a meaningful way, first by naming the landforms and second by explaining the significance of the landforms.

Only a mini-conclusion is missing at the end to tie the answer together, so it gets 7 marks.

For SPaG, the answer is given 3 marks – spelling, syntax, and paragraphing are all good.

On your marks

Using the command word 'Evaluate'

- **In this section you'll learn how to tackle 6- and 8-mark questions that use 'Evaluate' as a command word.**

Question

Evaluate the evidence that suggests that global climate is currently changing.   **(8 marks + 3 marks for SPaG)**

1 Plan your answer

Before attempting to answer the question, remember to **BUG** it. That means:

✓ **Box** the command word.
✓ **Underline** the following:
  - the theme
  - the focus
  - any evidence required
  - the number of examples needed.
✓ **Glance** back over the question to make sure you include everything in your answer.

Use the BUG example below to plan your own answer.

> **Remember!**
>
> The command word 'Evaluate' assesses AO2 (your knowledge and understanding of the topic) and AO3 (your ability to judge how strong the evidence is).

Command word: Evaluate means 'judge on its strengths and weaknesses'. So you need to decide whether evidence is strong or weak. 'Evaluate' requires a mini-conclusion.

Evidence: Support your answer with evidence from your own knowledge and understanding, such as shrinking glaciers and seasonal weather changes.

Evaluate the evidence that suggests that global climate is currently changing.   **(8 marks + 3 marks for SPaG)**

Theme: Climate change is linked to the Topic 2, Changing Climate, assessed in Paper 1, Section A of your exam. The question is compulsory.

Focus: You must explain the **evidence** that global climate is changing, and how reliable or strong it is.

Focus and number of examples: The focus is evidence for a changing global climate. For an 8-mark question, you need three well-explained and well-developed points. Each piece of evidence needs to be written in a paragraph.

Five steps to help you write top quality answers

The following five steps are used in this section to help you get the best marks.

1
Plan your answer – decide what to include and how to structure your answer.

2
Write your answer – use the answer spaces to complete your answer.

3
Mark your answer – use the mark scheme to self- or peer-mark your answer. You can also use this to assess sample answers in step 4 below.

4
Sample answers – sample answers show you how to maximise marks for a question.

5
Marked sample answers – these are the same answers as for step 4, but are marked and annotated so that you can compare them with your own answers.

How is SPaG assessed?

One 8-mark question on each of Papers 1 and 2 will assess your accuracy of spelling, punctuation, grammar and the use of specialist terminology (known as SPaG). In each of these questions, three marks are allocated as follows:

* High performance – 3 marks
* Intermediate performance – 2 marks
* Threshold performance – 1 mark.

Examiners mark SPaG based on your:

* spelling accuracy, including capitalisation
* punctuation – the use of commas, full stops and semi-colons. If reading an answer aloud leaves you gasping for breath, it needs more punctuation.
* syntax – the quality of your grammar
* paragraphing.

PEEL your answer

Use PEEL notes to structure your answer. This will help you to communicate your ideas to the examiner in the clearest way. PEEL has four stages.

* **P**oint – give at least three pieces of evidence for this question. Use sentences, not bullet points.
* **E**xplain – give reasons for each piece of evidence and how it shows climate is changing. Use sentence starters such as: 'This is because ...', 'One reason is ...'.
* **E**vidence – include details from named examples to support each piece of evidence.
* **L**ink – link back to the question about how reliable the evidence is, using PEE sentence starters. Finish with a one-sentence conclusion about how strong the evidence is that climate is changing.

 Tip

'Evaluate' means stating how strong each piece of evidence is

Don't just describe and explain. 'Evaluate' needs you to show if the research and evidence is strong or not.

For example, evidence of global climate change might be shown by shrinking glaciers. Then draw it together in a **mini-conclusion** – it need only be a sentence or two.

Planning grid

Use this planning grid to help you write high-quality paragraphs. Remember to include links to show how your points relate to each other and to the question. Note that this is an 8-mark question, so needs three PEE paragraphs.

Note that there is a fourth row to help you focus on the word 'Evaluate'. In this question, remember to **evaluate the evidence**.

(?) Question recap

Evaluate the evidence that suggests that global climate is currently changing.

	PEE Paragraph 1	PEE Paragraph 2	PEE Paragraph 3
Point			
Explanation			
Evidence *(from your own knowledge)*			
Link back to the question – a mini-conclusion (evaluate the evidence)			

2 Write your answer

Evaluate the evidence that suggests that global climate is currently changing.

(8 marks + 3 marks for SPaG)

Remember!

'Evaluate' assesses AO2 (knowledge and understanding) and AO3 (application).

_____

_____

_____

_____

_____

_____

_____

_____

_____

_____

_____

_____

_____

_____

_____

Strengths of the answer	
Ways to improve the answer	

Answer level		**Mark out of 8**	
SPaG level		**Mark out of 3**	

3 Mark your answer

1. To help you to identify well-structured points in the answer, highlight the:

   - points in red   • explanations in orange   • evidence in blue
   - underline any links to the question that show evaluation

2. Use the mark scheme below to decide what mark to give. 8-mark questions are not marked using individual points, but instead you should choose a level and a mark based upon the quality of the answer as a whole.

Level	Marks	Description	Examples
3 (Well-developed / Thorough)	7–8	**For AO2** • Thorough understanding of the topic • Information is relevant and detailed **For AO3** • Thorough analysis of the question title • Ideas are well developed with clear evidence • Well-developed lines of reasoning • Clear and logically structured argument	• *IPCC research shows that average global sea level has risen by 10–20 cm since 1920.* • *This is probably due to rising global temperatures, which melt ice caps, from which more water goes into the sea.* • *This is likely to be reliable evidence as the IPCC consists of thousands of the world's best scientists.*
2 (Developed / Reasonable)	4–6	**For AO2** • Reasonable understanding of the topic • Information is generally relevant with some detail **For AO3** • Some analysis of the question title • Ideas are developed with some evidence • Some lines of reasoning present • Argument is presented with some structure	• *Scientists show that global sea levels have risen in the past 100 years.* • *This is due to global warming, which increases temperatures and melted ice caps and glaciers, which go into the sea.* • *We know sea level is rising because countries with coastlines are getting flooded.*
1 (Simple/ Basic)	1–3	**For AO2** • Basic understanding of the topic • Information is often irrelevant or in little detail **For AO3** • Little or no analysis of the question title • No development of ideas; limited evidence • Unclear lines of reasoning • Argument is basic with little structure	• *World temperatures are going up all the time and winters are getting warmer.* • *Global warming is making the seasons different and there are more floods.* • *Scientists think more floods and storms are caused by global warming.*
	0	No accurate response	

4 Sample answers

Read the two sample answers on page 44. Go through each one using the three colours in step 3, including underlining any evaluative points. Use the level descriptions to decide how many marks each answer is worth. Remember to give a mark for SPaG.

Sample answer 7

Many sources of evidence show how climate is changing. Temperatures have risen globally since the nineteenth century by about 0.8°C. This is probably due to carbon emissions of greenhouse gases like CO_2 from burning of fossil fuels.

Temperatures seem to be getting warmer all the time, so that sea level will carry on rising. Already some islands in the Pacific have been flooded and countries like Bangladesh have severe floods because much of the country is very low-lying. Glaciers in mountains like the Himalayas have been melting because temperatures are rising, so that this all goes to the sea via rivers and makes sea level rise.

Another piece of evidence is that the seasons seem to be changing, so that spring is earlier and winters are not so cold as they were and have less snow. Birds now migrate earlier than they did and their nests are being built nine days earlier than forty years ago. So that all seems to mean that there is a lot of evidence that climate is changing.

Strengths of the answer		Ways to improve the answer	
Answer level		Mark		SPaG Level		Mark	

Sample answer 8

Globally the climate is warming, with evidence to prove that this is the case. Global temperatures are 1°C warmer than they were 100 years ago because greenhouse gas emissions have increased. It is hard to know exactly what temperatures were like in 1900, and more people and organisations record the weather now than at that time, but there were thermometers, just fewer of them. So some of the evidence could be questionable just because there are more recordings.

Even if temperature recordings are not completely reliable, there is a lot of evidence to show that sea level is rising globally by about 20 cm in 100 years, partly because ocean water expands when it warms and so it rises. Many coastal areas are flooding more now, so it is a global process and not just evidence from one place.

Other evidence that shows that temperatures are rising comes from retreating glaciers and ice sheets because they are melting. Many glaciers have been photographed for over 100 years, and many in the Alps and on Greenland show that they have retreated a long way from where they were.

Strengths of the answer		Ways to improve the answer	
Level		Mark		SPaG Level		Mark	

5 Marked sample answers

The sample answers on page 44 are marked below. The text has been highlighted to show how well each answer has structured points:

- points in red
- explanations in orange
- evidence in blue
- judgements are underlined. These are important for reaching Level 3 on questions using the command word 'Evaluate'.

 Question recap

Evaluate the evidence that suggests that global climate is currently changing.

Marked sample answer 7

Explanation – gives a reason for warming of the global climate

Point – quantifies the amount of warming

Point – offers further evidence

Explanation – gives a reason for flooding in many countries

Point – gives further evidence for climate change

Explanation – gives a reason for glaciers melting

Evidence – discusses retreating glaciers as evidence for rising sea levels

Point – gives further evidence for climate change (winters less cold)

Evidence – extends the point using the example of bird migrations

> Many sources of evidence show how climate is changing. Temperatures have risen globally since the nineteenth century by about 0.8°C. This is probably due to carbon emissions of greenhouse gases like CO_2 from burning of fossil fuels.
>
> Temperatures seem to be getting warmer all the time, so that sea level will carry on rising. Already some islands in the Pacific have been flooded and countries like Bangladesh have severe floods because much of the country is very low-lying. Glaciers in mountains like the Himalayas have been melting because temperatures are rising, so that this all goes to the sea via rivers and makes sea level rise.
>
> Another piece of evidence is that the seasons seem to be changing, so that spring is earlier and winters are not so cold as they were and have less snow. Birds now migrate earlier than they did and their nests are being built nine days earlier than forty years ago. So that all seems to mean that there is a lot of evidence that climate is changing.

 Examiner feedback

Examiners see many answers of this kind. This candidate knows a lot and has learned facts and figures. The answer is a problem, though, because there is no evaluation. The candidate needs to ask themselves – 'What's the evidence that glaciers are melting, and is it reliable? How do I know it's reliable?'

The answer is therefore a mix of levels.

- It almost reaches Level 3 for knowledge and understanding about climate change and global warming.
- Explanations are mid-Level 2 because they do not always link to warming climate (e.g. flooding in Bangladesh is explained because it is low lying, not because of sea level change).
- However, there is no evaluation, an essential feature for high Level 2 or Level 3.

Faced with this, examiners have to do a 'best fit' or a kind of average. The examiner gives this low Level 2 overall with 4 marks. SPaG is high quality, so 3 marks were awarded.

Marked sample answer 8

Question recap

Evaluate the evidence that suggests that global climate is currently changing.

Explanation – briefly explains the increase

Point – makes the point about increasing temperatures

Globally the climate is warming, with evidence to prove that this is the case. Global temperatures are 1°C warmer than they were 100 years ago because greenhouse gas emissions have increased. It is hard to know exactly what temperatures were like in 1900, and more people and organisations record the weather now than at that time, but there were thermometers, just fewer of them. So some of the evidence could be questionable just because there are more recordings.

Even if temperature recordings are not completely reliable, there is a lot of evidence to show that sea level is rising globally by about 20 cm in 100 years, partly because ocean water expands when it warms and so it rises. Many coastal areas are flooding more now, so it is a global process and not just evidence from one place.

Other evidence that shows that temperatures are rising comes from retreating glaciers and ice sheets because they are melting. Many glaciers have been photographed for over 100 years, and many in the Alps and on Greenland show that they have retreated a long way from where they were.

Evaluation – gives one reason why temperature readings may not be accurate

Evaluation – extends the evaluation by referring to the volume of temperature recordings

Point – makes a second point about rising sea level

Explanation – gives a reason for this

Evaluation – shows that this is probably reliable as many places experience the same thing

Point – makes the point about retreating glaciers

Evaluation – refers to the reliability of photos taken over a long time to show change

Explanation – explains this point

 Examiner feedback

This is a top-quality answer. Notice that this candidate has shown less knowledge and understanding (AO2) than the candidate in sample answer 7, but that nearly half of the answer is spent showing whether the evidence for change is reliable or not (AO3). That's what you need to do in a question with 'Evaluate' as the command word. Spend as much time on evaluating as you do in showing your knowledge and understanding.

The full 8 marks were awarded for the answer. SPaG is high quality, so 3 marks were awarded.

On your marks

Using the command 'How far do you agree'

- **In this section you'll learn how to tackle 6- and 8-mark questions that use the command 'How far do you agree'.**

Five steps to help you write top quality answers

Follow the five steps on page 16 to help you get the best marks.

Question

Study **Fig. 1**, showing a street scene in Rocinha Favela, a low-income housing area in Rio de Janeiro.

Fig. 1

'For those who live in low-income areas of mega-cities such as Rio de Janeiro, life presents far more problems than benefits'.

How far do you agree with this statement?

(8 marks + 3 marks for SPaG)

Remember!

The command 'How far do you agree' assesses AO2 (your knowledge and understanding of the topic, including what you see in the photo) and AO3 (your ability to apply what you know and understand, and to argue how far you agree with the statement).

1 Plan your answer

Before attempting to answer the question, remember to **BUG** it. Use the guidelines on page 16. Annotate it in the margin.

'For those who live in low-income areas of mega-cities such as Rio de Janeiro, life presents far more problems than benefits'.

How far do you agree with this statement?

(8 marks + 3 marks for SPaG)

PEEL your answer

Use PEEL notes to structure your answer.

- **P**oint – give at least three pieces of evidence from your mega-city study. Use sentences, not bullet points.
- **E**xplain – give reasons for each piece of evidence and how it illustrates problems or benefits of living in low-income areas. Use sentence starters such as: 'This is because …', 'One reason is …'.
- **E**vidence – include details from named examples of your mega-city to support each piece of evidence.
- **L**ink – link back to the question about whether living in low-income areas of mega-cities presents more problems than benefits. Finish with a one-sentence conclusion about your judgement.

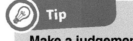

Make a judgement

Don't just describe and explain. If the question asks you 'How far do you agree', it wants you to make a judgement. Is it true that life presents far more problems than benefits for those living in low-income areas of mega-cities? Or not? One way to give a judgement is in a **mini-conclusion** – it need only be a sentence or two.

Planning grid

Use this planning grid to help you write high-quality paragraphs. Remember to include links to show how your points relate to each other and to the question. Note that there is a fourth row to help you link back to the command 'How far do you agree'.

	PEE Paragraph 1	PEE Paragraph 2	PEE Paragraph 3
Point			
Explanation			
Evidence			
Link back to the question – a mini-conclusion *(How far do you agree?)*			

2 Write your answer

'For those who live in low-income areas of mega-cities such as Rio de Janeiro, life presents far more problems than benefits.'

How far do you agree with this statement?

(8 marks + 3 marks for SpaG)

_____

_____

_____

_____

_____

_____

_____

_____

_____

_____

_____

_____

_____

_____

_____

_____

_____

Strengths of the answer		
Ways to improve the answer		
Answer level		**Mark out of 8**	
SPaG level		**Mark out of 3**	

Remember!

As with all 8-mark questions in Papers 1 and 2, you need to give a mark out of 3 for SPaG.

3 Mark your answer

1. To help you to identify well-structured points in the answer, highlight the:

   - points in red   • explanations in orange   • evidence in blue
   - underline any links to the question that show assessment of the statement. These might support one side of the argument or balance it before reaching a conclusion.

Remember!

Remember to give a mark for SPaG. The criteria can be found on page 31.

2. Use the mark scheme below to decide what mark to give. 8-mark questions are not marked using individual points, but instead you should choose a level and a mark based upon the quality of the answer as a whole.

Level	Marks	Description	Examples
3 (Well-developed / Thorough)	7–8	**For AO2** • Thorough understanding of the topic • Information is relevant and detailed **For AO3** • Thorough analysis of the question title • Ideas are well developed with clear evidence • Well-developed lines of reasoning • Clear and logically structured argument	• *In Rio, a third of homes have no electricity (or have illegal hook-ups from wires like the ones in the photo) and half have no sewage connections.* • *One reason is that favelas like Rocinha are growing so quickly that the city council cannot keep pace with population growth.* • *This shows the statement is true because electricity and sewerage connection are basics for a reasonable life. But there are benefits, such as provision of schooling.*
2 (Developed / Reasonable)	4–6	**For AO2** • Reasonable understanding of the topic • Information is generally relevant, with some detail **For AO3** • Some analysis of the question title • Ideas are developed with some evidence • Some lines of reasoning present • Argument is presented with some structure	• *Cities like Rio often have no water or sewerage connections, and electricity in the photo looks unsafe too.* • *This is because people are poor and cannot afford water or electricity bills.* • *So the statement is true because most people do not have a decent lifestyle with basics that we would take for granted.*
1 (Simple/ Basic)	1–3	**For AO2** • Basic understanding of the topic • Information is often irrelevant or in little detail **For AO3** • Little or no analysis of the question title • No development of ideas; limited evidence • Unclear lines of reasoning • Argument is basic with little structure	• *Developing cities have no water or sewage pipes and have many health problems from drinking bad water.* • *There are so many people that the city cannot keep pace with them all.* • *So the statement is right because life there is very hard and the city cannot support all those people.*
	0	No accurate response	

Sample answers

Read two sample answers below. Mark each one using the three colours in step 3 and underlining points that make assessments. Use the level descriptors to decide how many marks each answer is worth and a mark for SPaG.

Sample answer 9

I agree with the statement. Rio's favelas are growing so quickly that it is hard to keep pace with services needed like water. Rocinha has grown three times its size since 2010. It is better than it was because now houses are being built out of brick instead of timber and odd bits of metal, and they also have water and electricity. There are shops there and many services like health facilities that you would expect. But I agree with the statement because Rocinha is probably one of Rio's best favelas and there are many worse that do not have half the benefits that it has. You wouldn't choose to live there if you had more money so areas like that are still for low-income people, so I still think the statement is true.

Elsewhere Rio has squatter settlements, which are places where people just put together their own shacks illegally. Some of these shacks are on sloping land because nobody else wants to live there and they can be a long way from jobs in the city centre. But when rains come, people are vulnerable, because in 2010 over 200 people were killed in a landslide, which shows how the statement is true. This shows again how the statement is true, because it's the poor have to live there – people with jobs and decent incomes would never choose to live in places like that.

Strengths of the answer			Ways to improve the answer		
Answer level		Mark	SPaG level		Mark

Sample answer 10

I don't agree with the statement. It is true that people living in squatter settlements have a lot of problems like they don't have water supply or sewerage connections and when you walk down the street in the photo then you might be electrocuted as the wires don't look very safe. But cities have many jobs for people and so the people who have moved there from the countryside are often employed more than if they had stayed in rural areas. Many rural areas do not have schools and cities like Rio, which has plenty of schools for all ages and maybe universities too. There are often hospitals and medical treatment in cities that you don't have in the countryside. So it's not perfect living in Rio but it can be better than a lot of places. So I don't agree with the statement.

Strengths of the answer			Ways to improve the answer		
Answer level		Mark	SPaG level		Mark

5 Marked sample answers

The sample answers on page 51 are marked below. The text has been highlighted to show how well each answer has structured points:

- points in red
- explanations in orange
- evidence in blue
- judgements are underlined. These are important for reaching Level 3 on questions using the command 'How far do you agree'.

Marked sample answer 9

Explanation – gives an explanation for the impact of this growth

Point – quantifies the growth of Rocinha

Evidence – uses the evidence of building materials

Evidence – uses further evidence of shops and health servieces

Judgement – makes a comparison to justify the choice

I agree with the statement. Rio's favelas are growing so quickly that it is hard to keep pace with services needed like water. Rocinha has grown three times its size since 2010. It is better than it was because now houses are being built out of brick instead of timber and odd bits of metal, and they also have water and electricity. There are shops there and many services like health facilities that you would expect. But I agree with the statement because Rocinha is probably one of Rio's best favelas and there are many worse that do not have half the benefits that it has. You wouldn't choose to live there if you had more money so areas like that are still for low-income people, so I still think the statement is true.

Judgement – makes a further statement to justify the choice

Point – mentions squatter settlements

Elsewhere Rio has squatter settlements, which are places where people just put together their own shacks illegally. Some of these shacks are on sloping land because nobody else wants to live there and they can be a long way from jobs in the city centre. But when rains come, people are vulnerable, because in 2010 over 200 people were killed in a landslide, which shows how the statement is true. This shows again how the statement is true, because it's the poor have to live there – people with jobs and decent incomes would never choose to live in places like that.

Explanation – explains squatter settlements

Evidence – uses evidence about land used by squatter settlements

Point – describes the vulnerability of people

Explanation – gives an explanation to illustrate

Judgement – gives one further supporting statement to justify the choice, though very similar to the second justification

---

✓ **Examiner feedback**

This candidate knows a lot and has a clear view of what living in a favela might be like. The points are well made and the extended points offer a lot of detail about favelas to support the answer. The candidate also justifies clearly why they have reached an opinion. The answer is generally Level 3 in quality. However, it is not perfect, as the answer is short on data.

The answer is Level 3 and the justification is sound, so it earns 7 marks. It is well written, so earns 3 marks for SPaG.

Marked sample answer 10

 Question recap

'For those who live in low-income areas of mega-cities such as Rio de Janeiro, life presents far more problems than benefits.'

How far do you agree with this statement?

Evidence – extends the point using evidence about electricity from the photo

Point – makes an illustrated point about squatter settlements

I don't agree with the statement. It is true that people living in squatter settlements have a lot of problems like they don't have water supply or sewerage connections and when you walk down the street in the photo then you might be electrocuted as the wires don't look very safe. But cities have many jobs for people and so the people who have moved there from the countryside are often employed more than if they had stayed in rural areas. Many rural areas do not have schools and cities like Rio, which has plenty of schools for all ages and maybe universities too. There are often hospitals and medical treatment in cities that you don't have in the countryside. So it's not perfect living in Rio but it can be better than a lot of places. So I don't agree with the statement.

Point – makes the point about employment in cities

Evidence – uses evidence of employment to compare cities and rural areas

Point – makes the point about education in cities

Evidence – uses the evidence of healthcare to extend the point further

Judgement – makes a single statement about living in Rio, though this is not a quality comparison

✓ **Examiner feedback**

This is a medium-quality answer. The candidate makes three valid points about living in squatter settlements (AO2) and extends it with some detail, but a named city occurs just once in the last sentence. Generic writing – without naming a place – is normally typical of Level 1 – so the candidate has saved themselves by naming Rio twice. The level of justification (AO3) is weak; there is no other named place to compare cities with, simply mentioning rural areas.

This candidate probably knows more than this, so some revision of a named city (perhaps with some named examples of a mega-city or data illustrating households with water supply, etc.) would have earned a higher level for AO2. Justification needs to be more than just a general statement at the end, in order to raise the level for AO3.

This answer was given 5 marks, in the middle of Level 2. It is fairly well written, though a more relaxed style than formal, so earns 2 marks for SPaG.

On your marks

Using the command 'To what extent'

- **In this section you'll learn how to tackle 6- and 8-mark questions that use the command 'To what extent'.**

Study **Fig. 2**, a map showing internal and international migration figures into London.

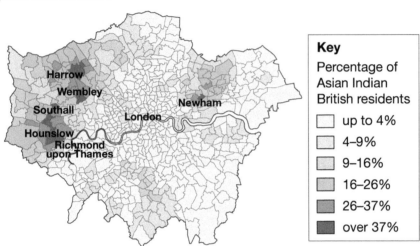

Key
Percentage of Asian Indian British residents

- [ ] up to 4%
- [ ] 4–9%
- [ ] 9–16%
- [ ] 16–26%
- [ ] 26–37%
- [ ] over 37%

Fig. 2 – A map showing the distribution of Asian Indian British people in London, 2011

> To what extent has international migration impacted upon the growth and character of cities in the UK?
>
> Use **Fig. 2** and your case study of a major city in the UK.
>
> **(6 marks)**

Five steps to help you write top quality answers

The following five steps are used in this section to help you get the best marks.

1

Plan your answer – decide what to include and how to structure your answer.

2

Write your answer – use the answer spaces to complete your answer.

3

Mark your answer – use the mark scheme to self- or peer-mark your answer. You can also use this to assess sample answers in step 4 below.

4

Sample answers – sample answers show you how to maximise marks for a question.

5

Marked sample answers – these are the same answers as for step 4, but are marked and annotated so that you can compare them with your own answers.

① Plan your answer

Before attempting to answer the question, remember to **BUG** it. Use the guidelines on page 16. Annotate it in the margin.

> To what extent has international migration impacted upon the growth and character of cities in the UK?
>
> Use **Fig. 2** and your case study of a major city in the UK.
>
> **(6 marks)**

PEEL your answer

Use PEEL notes to structure your answer. Use the guidelines on page 17 to help you.

Planning grid

Use this planning grid to help you write high-quality paragraphs. Remember to include links to show how your points relate to each other and to the question. Note that there is a fourth row to help you link back to the command 'To what extent'.

	PEE Paragraph 1	PEE Paragraph 2
Point		
Explanation		
Evidence *(from the map or your own knowledge)*		
Link back to the question – a mini-conclusion *(To what extent do you agree?)*		

 Tip

Make a judgement

Don't just describe and explain. If the question asks you 'To what extent?', it wants you to make a judgement . For example 'To what extent have the impacts of rainforest clearance been negative?' wants you to say whether rainforest clearance is positive or negative, or how big impacts have been (e.g. number of hectares cleared or species affected). One way to give a judgement is in a **mini-conclusion** – it need only be a sentence or two.

2 Write your answer

To what extent has international migration impacted upon the growth and character of cities in the UK?

Use **Fig. 2** and your case study of a major city in the UK.

(6 marks)

_____

_____

_____

_____

_____

_____

_____

_____

_____

_____

_____

_____

Strengths of the answer	
Ways to improve the answer	

Level		Mark	

Remember!

The command 'To what extent' assesses AO2 (your knowledge and understanding of the topic) and AO3 (your ability to apply your knowledge and understanding).

3 Mark your answer

1. To help you to identify well-structured points in the answer, highlight the:

   • points in red

   • explanations in orange

   • evidence in blue

   • underline any judgements.

2. Use the mark scheme below to decide what mark to give. Six-mark questions are not marked using individual points, but instead you should choose a level and a mark based upon the quality of the answer as a whole.

Level	Marks	Description	Examples
3 (Well-developed / Thorough)	7–8	**For AO2** • Thorough understanding of the topic • Information is relevant and detailed **For AO3** • Thorough analysis of the question title • Ideas are well developed with clear evidence • Well-developed lines of reasoning • Clear and logically structured argument	• *The impacts of immigration have been great, especially on the culture of UK cities. In Bradford, the Curry Mile attracts tourists as well as increasing the range of foods in the city.* • *Figure 2 shows that immigrants from particular countries, religions or cultures tend to live in areas close to each other, creating suburbs like Southall in West London.*
2 (Developed / Reasonable)	4–6	**For AO2** • Reasonable understanding of the topic • Information is generally relevant with some detail **For AO3** • Some analysis of the question title • Ideas are developed with some evidence • Some lines of reasoning are present • Argument is presented with some structure	• *Immigration has been the reason for half the recent growth of cities such as London. In London, over 200 languages are spoken.* • *Figure 2 shows that immigrants often settle in suburbs where there are cultural or ethnic groups like their own.*
1 (Simple/ Basic)	1–3	**For AO2** • Basic understanding of the topic • Information is often irrelevant or in little detail **For AO3** • Little or no analysis of the question title • No development of ideas; limited evidence • Unclear lines of reasoning • Argument is basic with little structure	• *East London has a lot of immigrants living there so the city is growing.* • *Immigrants often live in the same sorts of areas, where they have their own shops or mosques, and they like living there.*
	0	No accurate response	

4 Sample answers

Read the two sample answers below. Go through them using the three colours in step 3, including underlining any judgements. Judgements are needed to meet the requirements of the command 'To what extent'. Use the level descriptions to decide how many marks each answer is worth.

Question recap

To what extent has international migration impacted upon the growth and character of cities in the UK?

Use **Fig. 2** and your case study of a major city in the UK.

Sample answer 11

Half of London's population growth in recent years has been migrants from overseas, from countries such as India in Figure 2, because of the jobs available there such as in construction and financial services. International migration has also affected Birmingham because people from over 100 countries have settled there. Only 53% of the people living in Birmingham now are White British residents.

Like the map in Figure 2, many immigrants have changed the character of the parts of inner cities where they live, because you would find restaurants, shops or places of worship in areas where they live. This changes the culture in cities and there are festivals like the Notting Hill Carnival in London. So immigration has had a big effect on cities.

Strengths of the answer	
Ways to improve the answer	
Level		Mark	

Sample answer 12

Cities like Birmingham are growing fast because of immigrants from other countries. There are jobs in Birmingham which attract people to live there. It has meant that there is pressure on jobs and housing but Birmingham gains because there are also new restaurants and festivals which helps the city's image. When migrants arrive they look for work anywhere, but when they get jobs, then their families come and join them, so that's what makes the population go up so quickly.

Strengths of the answer	
Ways to improve the answer	
Level		Mark	

5 Marked sample answers

The sample answers are marked below. The text has been highlighted to show how well each answer has structured points:

- points in red   • explanations in orange   • evidence in blue
- judgements are underlined. They are important for reaching Level 3 on questions using the command 'To what extent'.

Marked sample answer 11

Evidence – example of India illustrates the point

Point – quantifies the amount of population growth due to immigration

Explanation – gives the reason for immigration (employment)

Point – quantifies the extent of immigration from different countries

Evidence – evidenced with the example of data from Birmingham

Point – answers 'changing character of cities'

Explanation –explains how the character is changed, with examples

Evidence – illustrates the point with an example

Judgement – about how immigration changes the city

Half of London's population growth in recent years has been migrants from overseas, from countries such as India in Figure 2, because of the jobs available there such as in construction and financial services. International migration has also affected Birmingham because people from over 100 countries have settled there. Only 53% of the people living in Birmingham now are White British residents.

Like the map in Figure 2, many immigrants have changed the character of the parts of inner cities where they live, because you would find restaurants, shops or places of worship in areas where they live. This changes the culture in cities and there are festivals like the Notting Hill Carnival in London. So immigration has had a big effect on cities.

 Examiner feedback

The descriptors for Level 3 apply to this answer as follows:

For AO2

- 'Thorough understanding of the topic' and 'Information is relevant and detailed'.
- The candidate mentions reasons for growth and the changing character of Birmingham. A source country is named, with an example of cultural events resulting from immigration. There is little mention of Figure 2.

For AO3

- 'Ideas are well developed with clear evidence' with 'Well-developed lines of reasoning' to form a 'Clear and logically structured argument'.
- The candidate explains London's growth and changing character. A source country is named and data are used, with an example of a cultural event.

However, the judgement is weaker than that needed for a top Level 3, so it gets 5 marks

Marked sample answer 12

Question recap

To what extent has international migration impacted upon the growth and character of cities in the UK?

Use **Fig. 2** and your case study of a major city in the UK.

Point – a simple point explains the growth of cities

Explanation – briefly explains the reason for growth, but without examples

Explanation – explains how jobs help to explain immigration, but without examples

Cities like Birmingham are growing fast because of immigrants from other countries. There are jobs in Birmingham which attract people to live there. It has meant that there is pressure on jobs and housing but Birmingham gains because there are also new restaurants and festivals which helps the city's image. When migrants arrive they look for work anywhere, but when they get jobs, then their families come and join them, so that's what makes the population go up so quickly.

Point – helps to answer the part of the question about changing character of cities

Explanation – revisits the explanation for growth of population

Evidence – shows evidence of the benefit of restaurants and festivals

Examiner feedback

The descriptors for Level 2 just about applies to this answer, as follows:

For AO2

- *'Reasonable understanding of the topic'* – the candidate names Birmingham and understands how immigration explains its rapid population growth. The candidate understands impacts of immigration (food and festivals), but there are no named examples as required for Level 3.

For AO3

- *'Some lines of reasoning are present'* and *'Argument is presented with some structure'* is evidence of Level 2. However, there's no judgement. Overall, the answer gains 3 marks.

On your marks

Using the command word 'Justify'

- **In this section you will learn how to prepare for 12-mark questions in Paper 3, which use the command word 'Justify'.**

What's different about Paper 3?

Paper 3 is different from Papers 1 and 2.

- Paper 3 is called 'Geographical Explorations' and consists of a decision-making exercise (DME) about a geographical issue. It could be based around any topic or combination of topics in the specification. It will probably be about a place that you haven't studied but it assesses your ability to read and interpret the resources not your knowledge of a particular place.
- The exam paper is divided into four questions (shown in the table below), each worth about a quarter of the total marks (60) – i.e. about 15.
- Most questions will test your understanding of the information in the Resource Booklet. But hold on to what you've revised for Papers 1 and 2, because Paper 3 also tests your knowledge and understanding (AO2) of topics from across the GCSE course that are linked to the issue. You will also need to apply this understanding (AO3).
- Some questions will involve calculations, so you can use a calculator.
- The paper also includes two 12-mark questions (as well as others for fewer marks), asking you to analyse and make a decision about the issue.
- The exam lasts for 1 hour 30 minutes and is worth 60 marks, including 3 marks for SPaG. So time is less pressured than for Papers 1 and 2.

The Resource Booklet

- The Resource Booklet will take time to read and it is essential to read it carefully.
- It will give you information about the issue, the place and prospects for the future. It will contain a mix of text, maps, photographs, graphs, tables of data and sometimes views and opinions about the issue.
- Use these resources to help you make sense of the issue.

Paper 3: Geographical Explorations

You'll be given a Resource Booklet.

Total marks: 60, including 3 marks for SPaG

Counts for: 30%

Time: 1 hour 30 minutes

Question 1
- Marked out of about 15, including one 6-mark question.
- These questions will be about the place and its geography.

Question 2
- Marked out of about 17, including one 12-mark question.
- These questions will be about the Resource Booklet and you'll need to interpret this in detail.

Question 3
- Marked out of about 13, including one 6-mark question.
- These questions will focus on an issue now or in the future.

Question 4
- Marked out of 15, consisting of one 12-mark question plus 3 marks for SPaG.
- You will have to analyse the proposal and will be asked to suggest your own ideas.

Decision-making is a process. The exam questions are organised in a sequence to follow this process.

- The issue is stated at the start of the Resource Booklet.
- The two most demanding parts of the exam will be the two 12-mark questions in Questions 2 and 4, where you'll have to analyse material and justify either a proposal in the Resource Booklet or devise your own.
- In Question 4, you are likely to be asked to make a proposal for the future.
- Your mark will depend on your reasons for justifying this proposal. There are no right or wrong proposals.
- It's marked using a mix of AO2 (knowledge and understanding) and AO3 (justifying your argument).

How to justify an argument in Question 4

To do well on this 12-mark question, your answer will need to:

- make a clear explanation of one proposal
- consider its impacts on the economy, people and environment
- weigh up its advantages and disadvantages
- make an overall judgement.

To make a choice, consider the following:

Economic impacts

- Will jobs increase and will they be higher skilled, higher-paid?
- Will it increase GDP?
- Will the area attract more investment?

Social impacts

- Will people's quality of life improve?
- Will there be better housing, health and education?

Environmental impacts

- Will air and water quality improve?
- Will wildlife be protected, conserved?
- Will the living environment be improved?

The mark scheme for the 12-mark question in Question 4

This mark scheme has four levels, instead of three.

- Level 1 = 1–3 marks
- Level 2 = 4–6 marks
- Level 3 = 7–9 marks
- Level 4 = 10–12 marks

Level 4 uses the word 'comprehensive' to describe top-quality answers, above the quality of Levels 1, 2 and 3 in the table on page 11. To reach Level 4, you must show:

For AO2
- Comprehensive understanding of the proposal

For AO3
- Comprehensive evaluation of the proposal
- Comprehensive interpretation of the Resource Booklet
- Comprehensive justification of how the proposal would help the place develop
- Well-developed ideas about any other proposals that would help the place develop
- Clear attempts to link the issue to parts of the GCSE course
- Well-developed lines of reasoning

Checklist for top-quality 12-mark answers

- Have you explained the proposal(s)?
- Have you justified your choice of proposal with two advantages and two disadvantages?
- Have you given evidence from the Resource Booklet to support your proposal?
- Have you included evidence from the GCSE course to support your proposal?

Writing a top quality answer

Read the sample answer on page 64 of a candidate's answer to the following Question 4 (you will find all the details of the question on page 117).

Question

Choose the option you think would be the most effective way for the Maldives to cope with the problem of rising sea level.

Using evidence from the separate Resource Booklet and your own understanding, explain why you reached this decision.

Using highlighters, pick out where the candidate has:

- justified their choice of proposal (AO3)
- used information that isn't in the Resource Booklet but the candidate has learned from the rest of the course (AO2).

Decide on a mark out of 12 for the answer and a mark out of 3 for SPaG. Check your marks with the marked example opposite.

 Question recap

Choose the option you think would be the most effective way for the Maldives to cope with the problem of rising sea level.

Using evidence from the separate Resource Booklet and your own understanding, explain why you reached this decision.

Sample answer 13

The Maldives government faces awesome challenges. The causes of climate change are not within its control. Tourist numbers are growing and having a big impact on the country (Figure 15). It needs to protect its population and tourist industry, as well as produce food and jobs. Option 1 can provide all these, but it won't be cheap.

Option 1 is best as it assumes that the Maldives continues to exist. It allows economic growth while protecting marine assets. The government would be able to attract tourist-related industries and benefit from the economic multiplier from new jobs. It could invest in sea walls to prevent islands and Malé, the capital, from destruction caused by rising sea levels. The impacts of climate change are enormous and, if the Maldives is to survive, the government needs to act. Option 1 is a start – the Maldives survives only if this option is taken up.

Environmentally, Option 1 is costly. Figure 13 shows the capital lies on one island, and saving that must be a priority. But other islanders depend on the sea, from fishing to tourism (Figure 10). If protected, the Maldives has potential for eco-tourism, as people would want to see coral reefs, which are disappearing globally as coral bleaching takes place. This can only happen if Option 1 is chosen.

I rejected Option 2, though it ought to be something the government does anyway. The potential for renewable energy is massive (solar, wind). But it's like fighting fire with petrol. Unless the strategies in Option 1 are developed, there won't be any islands left on which to establish any renewable energies.

I rejected Option 3 because it's defeatist and the Maldives would cease to exist. Whatever was not lost to rising sea levels would be taken over by Saudi Arabia. I can't imagine the tourist hotels being happy with this option, nor can I imagine the global uproar if we lose something as precious as the Maldives anyway. The UN ought to get involved.

To conclude, Option 1 is best. In fact, it is the only option if we want the Maldives to continue as a country.

Marked sample answer 13

The sample answer has been marked below. The text has been highlighted to show how well it has structured points:

- <u>introduction</u> and <u>conclusions</u> are underlined
- parts of the argument (AO3) in red
- evidence from the Resource Booklet in blue
- information learned from the rest of the course (AO2) in orange.

<u>The Maldives government faces awesome challenges.</u> The causes of climate change are not within its control. <u>Tourist numbers are growing and having a big impact on the country (Figure 15). It needs to protect its population and tourist industry, as well as produce food and jobs. Option 1 can provide all these, but it won't be cheap.</u>

Option 1 is best as it assumes that the Maldives continues to exist. It allows economic growth while protecting marine assets. The government would be able to attract tourist-related industries and benefit from the economic multiplier from new jobs. It could invest in sea walls to prevent islands and Malé, the capital, from destruction caused by rising sea levels. The impacts of climate change are enormous and, if the Maldives is to survive, the government needs to act. <u>Option 1 is a start – the Maldives survives only if this option is taken up.</u>

Environmentally, Option 1 is costly. Figure 13 shows the capital lies on one island, and saving that must be a priority. But other islanders depend on the sea, from fishing to tourism (Figure 10). If protected, the Maldives has potential for eco-tourism, as people would want to see coral reefs, which are disappearing globally as coral bleaching takes place. <u>This can only happen if Option 1 is chosen.</u>

<u>I rejected Option 2,</u> though it ought to be something the government does anyway. The potential for renewable energy is massive (solar, wind). But it's like fighting fire with petrol. Unless the strategies in Option 1 are developed, there won't be any islands left on which to establish any renewable energies.

I rejected Option 3 because it's defeatist and the Maldives would cease to exist. Whatever was not lost to rising sea levels would be taken over by Saudi Arabia. I can't imagine the tourist hotels being happy with this option, nor can I imagine the global uproar if we lose something as precious as the Maldives anyway. The UN ought to get involved.

<u>To conclude, Option 1 is best. In fact, it is the only option if we want the Maldives to continue as a country</u>

 Examiner feedback

This answer gains the full 12 marks, plus 3 marks for SPaG. It meets AO2 and AO3 well, and the quality of SPaG is very high.

GCSE 9-1 Geography OCR B
Practice Paper 1

Our Natural World

Time allowed: 1 hour 15 minutes
Total number of marks: 70 marks (including 3 marks for spelling, punctuation, grammar and specialist terminology (SPaG))

Instructions
Answer **all** questions in Section A and Section B.

Information
- Quality of extended responses will be assessed in questions marked with an asterisk (✷)
- Spelling, punctuation, grammar and specialist terminology will be assessed in questions marked with a pencil (✏)

Answer **all** the questions.

Question 1   Global Hazards

| 1 | a | | Study **Fig. 1** in the separate Resource Booklet [see page 119], two maps showing the effects of El Niño. |

| 1 | a | i | Name **one** type of extreme weather event associated with the occurrence of El Niño. |

(1)

_____

_____

| 1 | a | ii | Using **Fig. 1** and your own knowledge, outline the causes of the extreme weather conditions associated with El Niño. |

(4)

_____

_____

_____

_____

_____

_____

_____

_____

| 1 | b | | Study **Fig. 2** in the separate Resource Booklet [see page 119], a diagram of the structure of Earth. |

| 1 | b | i | Complete the table below to act as a key to **Fig.1**. |

Number	Layer
1	
2	
3	outer core
4	inner core

(2)

1 b ii Explain how the processes of plate tectonics are linked to the structure of Earth.

(6)

_____

_____

_____

_____

_____

_____

_____

_____

_____

_____

_____

Total for Question 1 = 13 marks

Question 2   Changing Climate

2 a Briefly describe the pattern of climate change from the beginning of the Quaternary period to the present day.

(2)

_____

_____

_____

_____

2 b State **one** effect of climate change.

(1)

_____

_____

| 2 | c | List **two** pieces of evidence that can be used to show the pattern of climate change from the start of the Quaternary period to the present day.

(2)

1 _____

_____

2 _____

_____

| 2 | d | Explain how evidence from the past gives a reliable indication of climate change over time.

(2)

_____

_____

_____

_____

| 2 | e | Study **Fig. 3** in the separate Resource Booklet [see page 120], photographs showing different causes of climate change.

Using **Fig. 3** and your own knowledge, justify the idea that climate change is not just the result of human actions.

(6)

_____

_____

_____

_____

_____

_____

_____

_____

_____

_____

_____

_____

_____

Total for Question 2 = 13 marks

Question 3   Distinctive Landscapes

| 3 | a | | Study **Fig. 4** in the separate Resource Booklet [see page 121], a map showing the major physical features of the British Isles.

| 3 | a | i | Complete the table below by adding the correct letter against each upland area.

Upland area	Letter
Grampians	
Lake District	
Snowdonia	

(2)

| 3 | a | ii | List **two** features of upland areas, like those in the table above, that make them distinctive.

(2)

_____

_____

_____

_____

| 3 | b | | Study **Fig. 5** in the separate Resource Booklet [see page 121], a photograph showing part of the lower course of a river.

| 3 | b | i | Identify **one** feature typical of the lower course of a river valley in **Fig. 5**.

(1)

_____

_____

| 3 | b | ii | Using **Fig. 5** and your own knowledge, explain how meanders contribute to the shape of the cross-section of a river valley in its lower course.

★

(8)

_____

_____

_____

_____

_____

_____

_____

_____

_____

_____

_____

_____

_____

_____

_____

_____

_____

Total for Question 3 = 13 marks

Question 4   Sustaining Ecosystems

4 **a**   Study **Fig. 6** in the separate Resource Booklet [see page 122], three climate graphs of global ecosystems.

4 **a** **i**   Complete the table below by writing the letter of the correct climate graph against each type of ecosystem.

Ecosystem type	Letter
Hot desert	
Rainforest	
Polar region	

(2)

4 **a** **ii**   Describe **two** features of the vegetation of the hot deserts

(2)

1 _____

_____

2 _____

_____

4 b Study **Fig. 7** in the separate Resource Booklet [see page 123], a diagram showing the food web in a tropical rainforest.

Using **Fig. 7**, complete the table below by adding **one** example in each blank cell. An example has already been added.

Levels in an ecosystem	Producers (plants)	Primary consumers (herbivores)	Secondary consumers (preditors)	Tertiary Consumers (top preditors)
Examples		Macaws		

(3)

4 c **CASE STUDY – an area of tropical rainforest**

Name of the area of tropical rainforest:

_____

Evaluate **one** attempt to manage sustainably an area of tropical rainforest you have studied.

(6)

_____
_____
_____
_____
_____
_____
_____
_____
_____
_____
_____
_____
_____

Total for Question 4 = 13 marks

Answer **all** the questions.

Question 5 Physical Geography Fieldwork

5 **a** As part of a GCSE physical geography enquiry a candidate sampled river sediment at different points downstream.

Study the table below, showing the data collected.

Location	1	2	3	4	5	6	7	8	9	10
River sediment size (cm)	22	19	21	14	17	13	12	7	8	3

5 **a** **i** Complete the dispersion graph below, using the data from the table above.

(1)

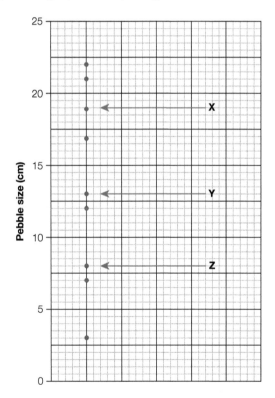

5 **a** **ii** On the graph, three values are labelled X, Y and Z. Complete the table below by writing the correct letter against each value.

Value	Letter
Median	
Lower quartile	
Upper quartile	

(2)

5 **a** **iii** Calculate the interquartile range. Show your working.

(2)

_____

_____

5 **a** **iv** Explain how the interquartile range can be a useful statistical technique when analysing fieldwork data.

(2)

_____

_____

_____

_____

5 **b**

＊

You carried out some physical geography fieldwork as part of your course.
Name the fieldwork:

_____

Evaluate the reliability of your conclusions.

(8)

Spelling, punctuation and grammar and the use of specialist technology

(3)

_____

_____

_____

_____

_____

_____

_____

_____

_____

_____

_____

_____

_____

_____

_____

Total for Question 5 = 18 marks

Practice papers
Set 1

GCSE 9-1 Geography OCR B
Practice Paper 2

People and Society

Time allowed: 1 hour 15 minutes
Total number of marks: 70 marks (including 3 marks for spelling, punctuation, grammar and specialist terminology (SPaG))

Instructions
Answer **all** questions in Section A and Section B.

Information
- Quality of extended responses will be assessed in questions marked with an asterisk (✱)
- Spelling, punctuation, grammar and specialist terminology will be assessed in questions marked with a pencil (✎)

Section A

Answer **all** the questions.

Question 1   Urban Futures

| 1 | a |

Study **Fig. 1** in the separate Resource Booklet [see page 124], a graph showing population change in a major world city.

| 1 | a | i |

What was the population of the city in 1970?

(1)

_____

| 1 | a | ii |

What was the approximate change in the population between 1950 and 2010?

(1)

_____

| 1 | a | iii |

Select which type of country this city is likely to be situated in.

Shade the correct circle.

A   Advanced country (AC)   ⬭

B   Low-income developing country (LIDC)   ⬭

(1)

| 1 | b |

Study **Fig. 2** in the separate Resource Booklet [see page 124], a factfile on Dharavi, a squatter settlement in the Indian city of Mumbai.

With the help of **Fig. 2**, explain why urban growth in EDCs (emerging and developing country) and LIDCs often leads to serious challenges for cities.

(4)

_____

_____

_____

_____

_____

_____

_____

_____

| 1 | c | **CASE STUDY – a city in EDC/LIDC** |

Name of the city in an EDC/LIDC:

_____

For a city in an EDC or an LIDC you have studied, evaluate the attempts of the
city to improve the living conditions of the inhabitants.

(6)

_____

_____

_____

_____

_____

_____

_____

_____

_____

_____

_____

_____

Total for Question 1 = 13 marks

Question 2   Dynamic Development

| 2 | a | Study **Fig. 3** in the separate Resource Booklet [see page 125], a table showing some economic and social measures of development.

| 2 | a | i | List **one** of the measures where a higher figure indicates a higher level of development.

(1)

_____

_____

| 2 | a | ii | List **one** of the measures where a lower figure indicates a higher level of development.

(1)

_____

_____

| 2 | a | iii | List **one** of the figures for Turkey that appears to be an anomaly or exception.

(1)

_____

_____

2 a iv Explain why is death rate not a good indicator of a country's level of development?

(2)

_____

_____

_____

_____

2 b **CASE STUDY – an LIDC**

✱

Name of the country:

_____

For an LIDC you have studied, explain how the country's pattern of trade may affect its development.

(8)

_____

_____

_____

_____

_____

_____

_____

_____

_____

_____

_____

_____

_____

_____

_____

_____

_____

_____

Total for Question 2 = 13 marks

Question 3   UK in the 21st Century

3 | **a**   Study **Fig. 4** in the separate Resource Booklet [see page 125], two pie charts showing the UK's employment structure in 1950 and 2015.

3 | **a** | **i**   Which **two** statements are true?

1   The primary sector is the smallest in both years.
2   The quaternary sector increased by the greatest proportion.
3   In 2015, the tertiary sector represented over three quarters of the total.
4   The secondary sector remained the largest between 1950 and 2015.

        A   1 and 2
        B   2 and 4
        C   1 and 3
        D   3 and 4

Write the correct letter in the box.

(1)

3 | **a** | **ii**   Describe how the employment structure of the UK changed between 1950 and 2015.

(4)

_____

_____

_____

_____

_____

_____

_____

_____

3 | **b** | **i**   Define what is meant by an 'economic hub'.

(2)

_____

_____

_____

_____

3 **b** **ii**   Describe how changes in **one** economic hub in the UK have affected the rest of the UK.

Name of UK economic hub:

_____

                                                                  (6)

_____

_____

_____

_____

_____

_____

_____

_____

_____

_____

_____

_____

_____

_____

_____

                                               Total for Question 3 = 13 marks

Question 4   **Resource Reliance**

4 **a**   Study **Fig. 5** in the separate Resource Booklet [see page 126], a map showing the relationship between the demand for and supply of water in the countries of Central Asia.

4 **a** **i**   Define the term 'water stress'?

                                                               (1)

_____

_____

4 **a** **ii**   Use **Fig. 5** to insert the correct information in the blank boxes in the following table.

Country	Water withdrawn (km³)	Water available (km³)
Tajikistan	10	
Turkmenistan	22	2
Kazakhstan		3
	1	29
Uzbekistan	38	12

                                                               (3)

4 a iii Name **one** country in **Fig. 5** that suffers water stress.

(1)

_____

_____

4 b **CASE STUDY – attempts to achieve food security in one country**

Name of country:

_____

4 b i Name **one** *past* attempt to achieve food security in this country at a national level.

(1)

_____

_____

4 b ii Name **one** *present* attempt to achieve food security in this country at a national level.

(1)

_____

_____

4 b iii Choose **either** the past attempt **or** the present attempt to achieve food security in this country. Investigate how effective this attempt was in achieving its aim.

(6)

_____

_____

_____

_____

_____

_____

_____

_____

_____

_____

_____

_____

_____

Total for Question 4 = 13 marks

Answer **all** the questions.

Question 5   Human Geography Fieldwork

| 5 | a |

Study **Fig. 6** in the separate Resource Booklet [see page 127], a photograph of part of Stoke Bishop in Bristol.

Annotate the copy of **Fig. 6** below to show **two** features of the built environment.

(2)

| 5 | b |

Study **Fig. 7** in the separate Resource Booklet [see page 127], a graph showing the percentage of different crimes committed over one year in Stoke Bishop.

| 5 | b | i |

Name the type of shown in **Fig. 7**.

(1)

_____

_____

| 5 | b | ii |

Which crime had the highest percentage recorded over the year in Stoke Bishop?

(1)

_____

_____

| 5 | b | iii |

What percentage of the total was vehicle crime?

(1)

_____

_____

5 **c** You carried out some human geography fieldwork as part of your course.

Name the fieldwork:

_____

Evaluate **one** technique you used to collect data.

(2)

_____

_____

_____

_____

5 **d**

★

Study **Figs 6**, **7**, **8, 9, 10** and **11** in the separate Resource Booklet [see pages 127–129], showing information from a GCSE human geography fieldwork investigation in Bristol.

Using evidence from **Figs 6**, **7, 8, 9** and **10**, write a conclusion to the investigation, which had the following title:
To what extent do the areas of Filwood and Stoke Bishop suggest that there are great social and environmental variations within the City of Bristol?

(8)

Spelling, punctuation and grammar and the use of specialist technology

(3)

_____

_____

_____

_____

_____

_____

_____

_____

_____

_____

_____

_____

_____

_____

_____

_____

Total for Question 5 = 18 marks

Practice paper
Set 1

GCSE 9-1 Geography OCR B
Practice Paper 3

Geographical Exploration

Time allowed: 1 hour 30 minutes
Total number of marks: 60 marks (including 3 marks for spelling, punctuation, grammar and specialist terminology (SPaG))

Instructions
Answer **all** the questions.

Information
- Quality of extended responses will be assessed in questions marked with an asterisk (★)
- Spelling, punctuation, grammar and specialist terminology will be assessed in questions marked with a pencil (✎)

Geographical Exploration

Answer **all** the questions.

Question 1

1 Study **Figs 1, 2, 3, 4, 5** and **6** in the separate Resource Booklet [see pages 130–135], information on UK population and housing.

1 a i Using **Fig. 1**, calculate the percentage increase in the UK's population from 2001 to 2015. Show your working.

(2)

_____

_____

_____

_____

1 a ii Using a *dotted line*, extend the current growth of population to when the total reaches 70 million.

(1)

1 **a** **iii** Estimate the year when the UK's population will reach 70 million.

(1)

_____

_____

1 **b** Using **Fig. 2**, describe the pattern of percentage growth in the UK's population between 2003 and 2013.

(3)

_____

_____

_____

_____

_____

1 **c** Study **Figs 3a** and **3b**, two maps showing the annual population growth and annual growth in housing in Great Britain, distorted in proportion to population.

Using evidence from **Figs 3a** and **3b**, describe what appears to be the relationship between the annual population growth and growth in housing from 2012 to 2014.

(4)

_____

_____

_____

_____

_____

_____

_____

_____

Total for Question 1 = 11 marks

Question 2

2 ✱

'The housing shortage is the result of natural increase in the country's population.'

To what extent do you agree with this statement?

Using information in **Figs 1, 2, 3, 4, 5** and **6**, give reasons for your answer.

(12)

_____

_____

_____

_____

_____

_____

_____

_____

_____

_____

_____

_____

_____

_____

_____

_____

_____

_____

_____

_____

_____

_____

Total for Question 2 = 12 marks

Question 3

3 Study **Figs 7** and **8** in the separate Resource Booklet [see pages 135 and 136], a bar chart showing the fastest growing cities in England and a map showing the main urban areas and green belts in England.

3 a i Name **one** of the fastest growing cities that does **not** have a green belt.

(1)

_____

_____

3 a ii To what extent does the pattern of green belts in England reflect the growth of the fastest growing cities in the country?

(4)

_____

_____

_____

_____

_____

_____

_____

_____

3 a iii Suggest **two** reasons for the pattern of the fastest growing cities in England.

(2)

1 _____

_____

2 _____

_____

3 b Study **Figs 9**, **10a** and **10b** in the separate Resource Booklet [see pages 137 and 138], an extract from an OS map showing part of the green belt in Bristol and two photographs showing disused industrial buildings in Bristol.

3 b i What is situated at 625796 on **Fig. 9**?

(1)

_____

_____

3 b ii There is an application for more housing to be built in the area around Harry Stoke in squares 6279 and 6278.

Using evidence from **Fig. 9**, suggest the advantages and disadvantages of building a new development at Harry Stoke on Bristol's green belt.

(6)

_____

_____

_____

_____

_____

_____

_____

_____

_____

_____

_____

_____

3 b iii Identify **two** features of the buildings in **Figs 10a** and **10b** that suggest that these are now brownfield sites.

(2)

1 _____

_____

2 _____

_____

3 **b** **iv** Explain the advantages and disadvantages of these and other brownfield sites for housing.

(6)

_____

_____

_____

_____

_____

_____

_____

_____

_____

_____

_____

Total for Question 3 = 22 marks

Question 4

4 'The UK has a Housing Crisis' was a headline to a recent newspaper article.

∗ Imagine you are the Government minister for housing and Planning.

Using supporting evidence from the separate Resource Booklet and your own understanding, write a report on the best strategy for coping with the UK's future housing needs.

(12)

Spelling, punctuation and grammar and the use of specialist terminology

(3)

_____

_____

_____

_____

_____

_____

_____

_____

_____

_____

_____

_____

_____

_____

_____

_____

_____

_____

_____

_____

_____

_____

_____

_____

_____

Total for Question 4 = 15 marks

Practice paper
Set 2

GCSE 9-1 Geography OCR B
Practice Paper 1

Our Natural World

Time allowed: 1 hour 15 minutes
Total number of marks: 70 marks (including 3 marks for spelling, punctuation, grammar and specialist terminology (SPaG))

Instructions
Answer **all** the questions in Section A and Section B.

Information
- Quality of extended responses will be assessed in questions marked with an asterisk (★)
- Spelling, punctuation, grammar and specialist terminology will be assessed in questions marked with a pencil (✎)

Answer **all** the questions.

Question 1   Global Hazards

| 1 | a | | Study **Fig. 1** in the separate Resource Booklet [see page 139], a diagram showing a plate boundary.

| 1 | a | i | Which of the following plate boundaries are shown in **Fig. 1**?

- **A**   Conservative
- **B**   Constructive
- **C**   Destructive

Write the correct letter in the box.

(1)

| 1 | a | ii | On the copy of **Fig.1** below, name and label the following features.

(4)

- Magma source
- Oceanic plate
- Subduction zone
- Trench

1 b Complete the table below, by giving the differences between shallow and deep earthquakes.

	Shallow earthquakes	Deep earthquakes
Frequency		
Direction of seismic waves		

(2)

1 c Explain how technological developments can reduce the risks from a type of tectonic hazard you have studied.

(6)

_____

_____

_____

_____

_____

_____

_____

_____

_____

_____

_____

_____

_____

_____

Total for Question 1 = 13 marks

Question 2   Changing Climate

2   Study **Fig. 2** in the Resource Booklet [see page 140], three photographs showing some impacts of climate change on the UK in the 21st century.

2 **a** **i**   Suggest which **three** impacts on the UK are shown in **Fig. 2**.

(3)

1 _____

_____

2 _____

_____

3 _____

_____

2 **a** **ii**   Describe **one** advantage and **one** disadvantage of climate change for the UK in the 21st century.

(2)

Advantage _____

_____

Disadvantage _____

_____

2 **b**   Assess the importance of volcanic eruptions and changes to solar output to climate change.

✱

(8)

_____

_____

_____

_____

_____

_____

_____

_____

_____

_____

_____

_____

_____

_____

_____

_____

_____

_____

Total for Question 2 = 13 marks

Question 3   Distinctive Landscapes

| 3 | a | Study **Fig. 3** in the separate Resource Booklet [see page 141], a diagram showing a coastal process.

| 3 | a | i | What is the name of this coastal process?

(1)

_____

| 3 | a | ii | On the copy of **Fig. 3** below, label the following features.

- Direction of coastal process
- Backwash
- Swash

(2)

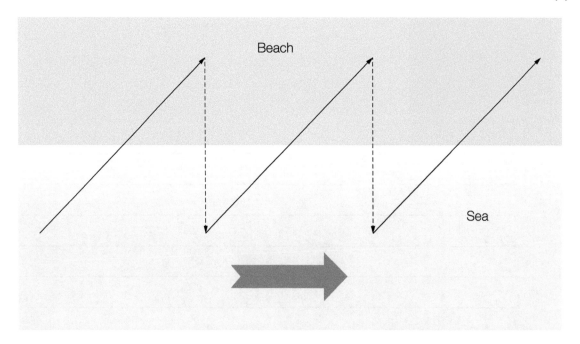

| 3 | b | Study **Fig. 4** in the separate Resource Booklet [see page 141], a photograph showing a coastal area in western Scotland.

| 3 | b | Using **Fig. 4** and your own knowledge, explain how deposition can affect the shape of the coastline.

(4)

_____

_____

_____

_____

_____

_____

_____

| 3 | c | **CASE STUDY – a coastal landscape in the UK**

Name of coastal landscape:

_____

Explain how management has affected the geomorphic processes along a stretch of coastal landscape in the UK you have studied.

(6)

_____

_____

_____

_____

_____

_____

_____

_____

_____

_____

_____

_____

Total for Question 3 = 13 marks

Question 4   Sustaining Ecosystems

| 4 | Study **Fig. 5** in the separate Resource Booklet [see page 142], a photograph showing a pond ecosystem.

| 4 | a | i | Identify a producer shown in **Fig. 5**.

(1)

_____

_____

| 4 | a | ii | Explain why ducks are good examples of consumers.

(1)

_____

_____

| 4 | a | iii | Imagine that the pond became polluted. Explain how this would impact on the ecosystem.

(2)

_____

_____

_____

_____

| 4 | a | iv | State where most decomposers live in the pond ecosystem.

(1)

_____

_____

| 4 | a | v | Explain the role of decomposers in nutrient recycling.

(2)

_____

_____

_____

_____

4 b   Examine the impact of human activity on *either* the Antarctic *or* the Arctic ecosystem.

Circle the **one** chosen.

Antarctic   Arctic

(6)

_____

_____

_____

_____

_____

_____

_____

_____

_____

_____

Total for Question 4 = 13 marks

Answer **all** the questions.

Question 5   Physical Geography Fieldwork

| 5 | a |

Study **Figs 6a** and **b** in the separate Resource Booklet [see page 142], two graphs showing the length and shape of river pebbles collected during a physical geography fieldwork investigation.

| 5 | a | i |

Explain why the methods of data presentation used are effective and mathematically accurate.

(2)

_____

_____

_____

_____

| 5 | a | ii |

Identify any anomalies in **Fig. 6b** that do not seem to fit the general pattern.

(1)

_____

_____

| 5 | a | iii |

Suggest a possible reason for these anomalies.

(1)

_____

_____

| 5 | b | i |

Explain **one** advantage of using a line graph to show the cross-section of a river valley.

(2)

_____

_____

_____

_____

| 5 | b | ii |

State what has to be avoided when deciding on the vertical scale of this line graph.

(1)

_____

_____

5 c

*

You carried out some physical geography fieldwork as part of your course.

Evaluate how you would change the type of data you collected and the methods you used to obtain your data in order to make your results and conclusions more reliable if you were to repeat the investigation.

(8)

Spelling, punctuation and grammar and the use of specialist terminology (3)

_____

_____

_____

_____

_____

_____

_____

_____

_____

_____

_____

_____

_____

_____

_____

_____

Total for Question 5 = 18 marks

GCSE 9-1 Geography OCR B
Practice Paper 2

People and Society

Time allowed: 1 hour 15 minutes
Total number of marks: 70 marks (including 3 marks for spelling, punctuation, grammar and specialist terminology (SPaG))

Instructions
Answer **all** the questions in Section A and Section B.

Information
- Quality of extended responses will be assessed in questions marked with an asterisk (⋆)
- Spelling, punctuation, grammar and specialist terminology will be assessed in questions marked with a pencil (✏)

Answer **all** the questions.

Question 1   Urban Futures

1 **a**   Study **Fig. 1** in the separate Resource Booklet [see page 143], a photograph showing a city street scene in northern England.

1 **a** **i**   List **two** features shown in **Fig. 1** that suggest that the population of the city is ethnically diverse.

(2)

1 _____

_____

2 _____

_____

1 **a** **ii**   Name **one** other feature of UK cities with ethnically diverse populations.

(1)

_____

_____

1 **a** **iii**   Explain ways in which a **named** city in an advanced country (AC) has been affected by having an ethnically diverse population.

Name of city:

_____

(4)

_____

_____

_____

_____

_____

_____

_____

_____

_____

1 **b** Discuss the reasons for rapid urban growth in large cities in EDCs. (6)

_____

_____

_____

_____

_____

_____

_____

_____

_____

_____

_____

_____

_____

Total for Question 1 = 13 marks

Question 2   Dynamic Development

2 **a** Study **Figs 2** and **3** in the separate Resource Booklet [see page 144], a location map and a factfile for the country of Burkina Faso in Africa.

2 **a** **i** There can be physical, economic and historical reasons why a country has a low level of development.

Write **one** statement taken from the factfile to illustrate each reason in the table below.

Physical reason	Economic reason	Historical reason

(3)

2 **a** **ii** Suggest how Burkina Faso's location in Africa may be an additional obstacle to the country's development.

(2)

_____

_____

_____

_____

| 2 | b | **CASE STUDY – an LIDC**

*   Name of an LIDC:

_____

For an LIDC you have studied, explore the extent to which the Millennium Development Goals have been achieved.

(8)

_____

_____

_____

_____

_____

_____

_____

_____

_____

_____

_____

_____

_____

_____

_____

_____

Total for Question 2 = 13 marks

Question 3   UK in the 21st Century

| 3 | a | Study **Fig. 4** in the separate Resource Booklet [see page 145], a diagram of a population model.

| 3 | a | i | What is the name of this population model?

(1)

_____

_____

3 a ii Complete the key below by adding 'Birth rate' and 'Death rate' to the correct symbol.

Key

[_____] _____

[_____] _____

(1)

3 b Study **Figs 5a** and **5b** in the separate Resource Booklet [see page 146], showing two population pyramids for the UK in 2001 and projected for 2021.

3 b i Describe **two** ways the population structure of the UK is projected to change from 2001 to 2021.

(2)

1 _____

_____

2 _____

_____

3 b ii According to the population pyramid for 2021, what stage of the population model in **Fig. 4** will the UK have reached by 2021?

(1)

_____

_____

3 c Study **Fig. 6** in the separate Resource Booklet [see page 147], a map showing the percentage of the population aged over 65 in England and Wales

Give **two** facts about the distribution of people aged over 65.

(2)

1 _____

_____

2 _____

_____

3 d Study **Fig. 7** in the separate Resource Booklet [see page 148], an extract from a newspaper article on the UK's ageing population.

Using **Fig. 7** and your own knowledge, examine the effects of and responses to the issue of the UK's ageing population.

(6)

_____

_____

_____

_____

_____

_____

_____

_____

_____

_____

_____

_____

Total for Question 3 = 13 marks

Question 4   Resource Reliance

4 a Study **Fig. 8** in the separate Resource Booklet [see page 148], a world map showing average daily calorie consumption.

4 a i Which of the following is considered the best average daily calorie intake for humans to ensure a healthy life?

        A 1–1000 calories
        B 1000 –1500 calories
        C 1500–2000 calories
        D 2000–2500 calories
        E 2500–3000 calories

Write the correct letter in the box.

(1)

4 a ii Name the **two** continents shown on **Fig. 8** with lowest average daily calorie intake.

(2)

1 _____

2 _____

4 a iii Explain how physical factors can influence the amount of food available for people to eat in certain parts of the world.

(4)

_____

_____

_____

_____

_____

_____

_____

4 b Explore technological developments aimed at achieving food security in a sustainable way.

(6)

_____

_____

_____

_____

_____

_____

_____

_____

_____

_____

_____

_____

Total for Question 4 = 13 marks

Answer **all** the questions.

Question 5   Human Geography Fieldwork

| 5 | a | i | Study the table below, showing some of the results of a human geography fieldwork investigation on the sphere of influence of a market town in the Midlands.

Complete the table by adding the **two** missing cumulative frequency totals.

Distance travelled to work or shop in the town	Number of people	Cumulative frequency (cumulative number of people)
5 miles	9	9
10 miles	7	
15 miles	3	
20 miles	1	20

(2)

| 5 | a | ii | Study **Fig. 9** in the separate Resource Booklet [see page 149], a cumulative frequency graph showing the results from the sphere of influence investigation.

Using **Fig. 9**, work out the interquartile range. Show your workings.

(2)

_____

_____

| 5 | a | iii | What do cumulative frequencies and quartiles tell you about this set of results?

(2)

_____

_____

_____

_____

| 5 | a | iv | Name **one** other graphical presentation technique that could be use to find the same information about this set of data.

(1)

_____

_____

5	b

★

Study **Figs 10 a, 10b, 11a, 11b** and **12** in the separate Resource Booklet [see pages 149–151], showing information from a GCSE human geography fieldwork investigation.

Using evidence from **Figs 10a, 10b, 11a, 11b** and **12**, write a conclusion to the investigation, which had the following title:

'The differences between the town centre and a retail park in Wrexham mean that the pattern of visits is not the same in both'.

(8)

Spelling, punctuation and grammar and the use of specialist terminology

(3)

_____

_____

_____

_____

_____

_____

_____

_____

_____

_____

_____

_____

_____

_____

_____

_____

_____

Total for Question 5 = 18 marks

GCSE 9-1 Geography OCR B
Practice Paper 3

Geographical Exploration

Time allowed: 1 hour 30 minutes
Total number of marks: 60 marks (including 3 marks for spelling, punctuation, grammar and specialist terminology (SPaG))

Instructions
Answer **all** the questions.

Information
- Quality of extended responses will be assessed in questions marked with an asterisk (⋆)
- Spelling, punctuation, grammar and specialist terminology will be assessed in questions marked with a pencil (✏)

Answer **all** the questions.

Question 1

| 1 | a | | Study **Fig. 1** in the separate Resource Booklet [see page 152], a computer-generated image showing a polar area.

| 1 | a | i | List **two** geographical facts suggested by this image.

(2)

1 _____

_____

2 _____

_____

| 1 | a | ii | Suggest why this image was produced for a newspaper article.

(2)

_____

_____

_____

_____

| 1 | b | | Study **Fig. 2** in the separate Resource Booklet [see page 152], a graph showing average global temperatures from 1880 to 2013.

| 1 | b | i | What was the range of temperature during this period?

(1)

_____

_____

| 1 | b | ii | Describe the trend of global temperatures during this period.

(3)

_____

_____

_____

_____

_____

_____

1 c Study **Fig. 3** in the separate Resource Booklet [see page 153], a photograph showing scientists working in the Arctic.

Suggest how the scientists' investigations could support or dispute the evidence shown in **Fig. 2**.

(2)

_____

_____

_____

_____

1 d Study **Fig 4** in the separate Resource Booklet [see page 153], three extracts from news articles about flooding in the UK.

Outline **one** cost and **one** benefit of providing sea defences in such areas.

(4)

_____

_____

_____

_____

_____

_____

_____

_____

1 e Study **Figs 5** and **6** in the separate Resource Booklet [see pages 154 and 155], a map and photograph showing Alkborough Flats and a factfile about the Alkborough Flats Tidal Defence Scheme, which is aimed at reducing coastal flooding.

Assess the benefits and disadvantages of the Alkborough Flats Tidal Defence Scheme.

(6)

_____

_____

_____

_____

_____

_____

_____

_____

_____

_____

_____

_____

Total for Question 1 = 20 marks

Question 2

2 '*Climate change has a range of social, economic and environmental impacts.*'

*

To what extent do you agree with this statement? Give reasons for your answer and include references to information in **Figs 1–6**.

(12)

_____

_____

_____

_____

_____

_____

_____

_____

_____

_____

_____

_____

_____

_____

_____

_____

_____

_____

_____

_____

_____

_____

_____

Total for Question 2 = 12 marks

Question 3

| 3 | a | Study **Figs 7** and **8** in the separate Resource Booklet [see pages 155 and 156], a map showing the location of and a factfile about the Maldives.

| 3 | a | i | Using **Fig. 7**, describe the location of the Maldives.

(2)

_____

_____

_____

_____

| 3 | a | ii | Using **Fig. 8**, give **one** _physical_ and **one** _human_ reason why the Maldives government is so concerned about the effects of climate change.

(2)

Physical _____

_____

Human _____

_____

| 3 | b | Study **Figs 9** and **10** in the separate Resource Booklet [see pages 156 and 157], a computer-generated image showing the Maldives shoreline and a graph showing different sectors of the Maldives' GDP.

| 3 | b | i | Calculate the percentage of the GDP that comes from tourism.

(1)

_____

_____

| 3 | b | ii |

Suggest **two** attractions in the Maldives that many tourists from the UK go on holiday to see.

(2)

1 _____

_____

2 _____

_____

| 3 | b | iii |

Suggest why agriculture is such a small part of the Maldives' GDP.

(2)

_____

_____

_____

_____

| 3 | c |

Study **Fig. 11** in the separate Resource Booklet [see page 157], a table showing methods of reducing carbon emissions. These methods also have economic benefits because they reduce spending.

Choose **one** of the methods listed in **Fig. 11** and explain how it would benefit the economy and the climate.

(4)

Method chosen:

_____

_____

_____

_____

_____

_____

_____

_____

_____

Total for Question 3 = 13 marks

Question 4

4   Study **Figs 12, 13** and **14** in the separate Resource Booklet [pages 158 and 159].

*

Three of the 200 inhabited islands in the Maldives have already been evacuated. At present rates, it is estimated that the rest of the country will be submerged within 30 years. **Fig. 12** outlines some of the issues the Maldives faces if the rise continues. The following three solutions have been suggested.

| **Option 1** |
| Build seawalls, like those shown in **Fig. 13**, and islands, such as Hulhamalé, shown in **Fig. 14**. |

| **Option 2** |
| Make the Maldives the first carbon-neutral country in the world by making it 100% dependent on renewable energy from solar panels and a wind farm. |

| **Option 3** |
| Lease the islands of Faafa Atol to Saudi Arabia in return for US$10 billion investment (three times the Maldives' GDP) to create an international city with a population of 1 million for wealthy people from around the world. The investment would pay for Option 1. |

Choose the option you think would be the most effective way for the Maldives to cope with the problem of rising sea level.

Using evidence from the separate Resource Booklet and your own understanding, justify your decision.

(12)

Spelling, punctuation and grammar and the use of specialist terminology   (3)

Option number chosen: _____

_____

_____

_____

_____

_____

_____

_____

_____

_____

_____

_____

Total for Question 4 = 15 marks

Fig. 1 – Two maps showing the effects of El Niño

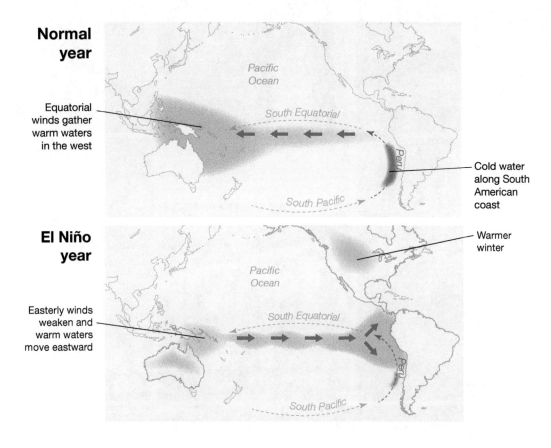

Normal year

Pacific Ocean

Equatorial winds gather warm waters in the west

South Equatorial

Peru

South Pacific

Cold water along South American coast

Warmer winter

El Niño year

Pacific Ocean

Easterly winds weaken and warm waters move eastward

South Equatorial

Peru

South Pacific

Fig. 2 – A diagram of the structure of Earth

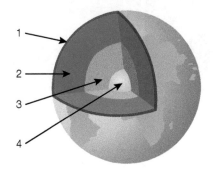

1
2
3
4

Fig. 3 – Photographs showing different causes of climate change

Fig. 4 – A map showing the major physical features of the British Isles

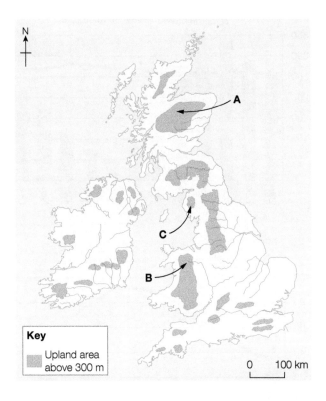

Key

Upland area above 300 m

0   100 km

Fig. 5 – A photograph showing part of the lower course of a river

Fig. 6 – Three climate graphs of global ecosystems

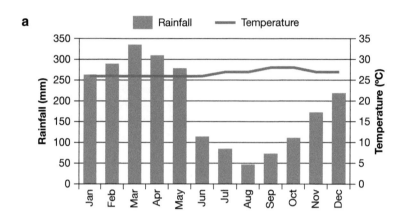

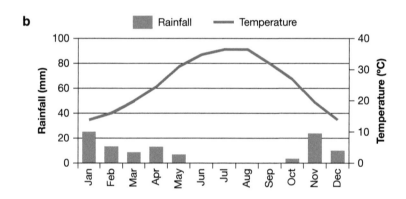

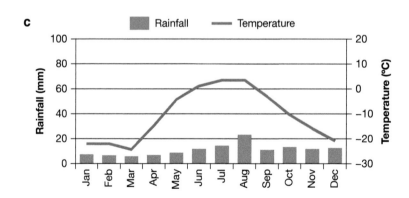

Fig. 7 – A diagram showing the food web in a tropical rainforest

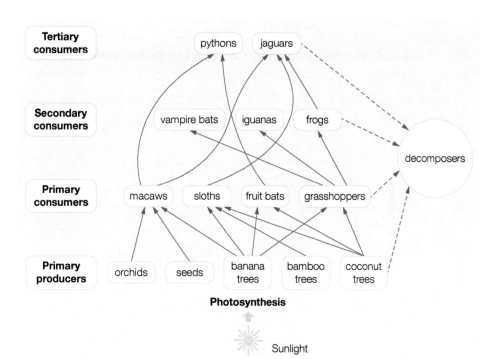

Fig. 1 – A graph showing population change in a major world city

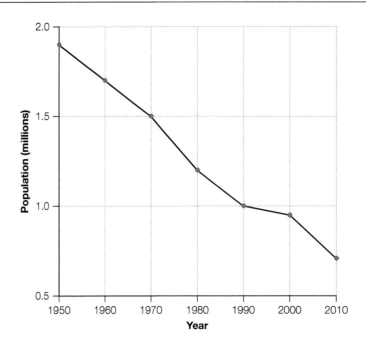

Fig. 2 – A factfile on Dharavi, a squatter settlement in the Indian city of Mumbai

People		Hygiene and health	
Population of Dharavi	Estimated 800 000–1 million	Number of individual toilets in Dharavi	1440
Area	2.39 km² (size of London's Hyde Park)	People per individual toilet	625
Population density	At least 330 000 people per km²	Women suffering from anaemia*	75%
Number of homes in Dharavi	60 000	Women with malnutrition	50%
People per home	13–17	Women with recurrent gastro-enteritis**	50%
Average size of home	10 m² (size of medium-sized bedroom)	Most common causes of death	Malnutrition, diarrhoea, dehydration, typhoid
		Education	
		Literacy rate in Dharavi	69% (Mumbai average is 91%)

* anaemia is a lack of iron leading to tiredness

** gastro-enteritis symptoms are diarrhoea and vomiting

Fig. 3 – A table showing some social and economic measures of development

---

Country	GNI per head (US$)	HDI	Birth rate (per 1000 per year)	Death rate (per 1000 per year)	Infant mortality (per 1000 live births per year)	Number of doctors (per 1000 people)	Literacy rate (%)	% of population with access to safe water
USA	55200	0.915	12.49	9.35	5.87	2.5	99.0	99
Japan	42000	0.891	7.93	9.51	2.08	2.3	99.0	100
UK	43430	0.907	12.17	9.35	4.38	2.8	99.0	100
Brazil	11530	0.755	14.46	6.58	18.60	1.9	92.6	98
Turkey	10830	0.761	16.33	5.88	18.87	1.70	95.0	100
China	7400	0.727	12.49	7.53	12.44	1.90	96.4	95
Nigeria	2970	0.514	37.64	12.90	72.70	0.40	59.6	69
Ivory Coast	1450	0.462	28.67	9.55	58.70	.01	43.1	82
Bangladesh	1080	0.570	21.14	5.61	44.09	.40	61.5	87
Zimbabwe	840	0.509	32.26	10.13	26.11	.10	86.5	77

Fig. 4 – Two pie charts showing the UK's employment structure in 1950 and 2015

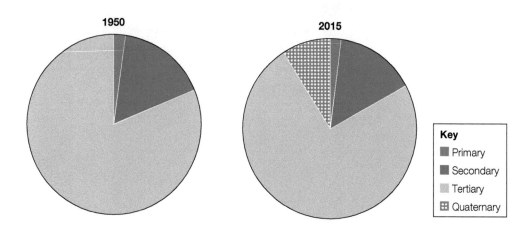

1950   2015

Key
■ Primary
■ Secondary
▨ Tertiary
▦ Quaternary

Fig. 5 – A map showing the relationship between the demand for and supply of water in the countries of Central Asia

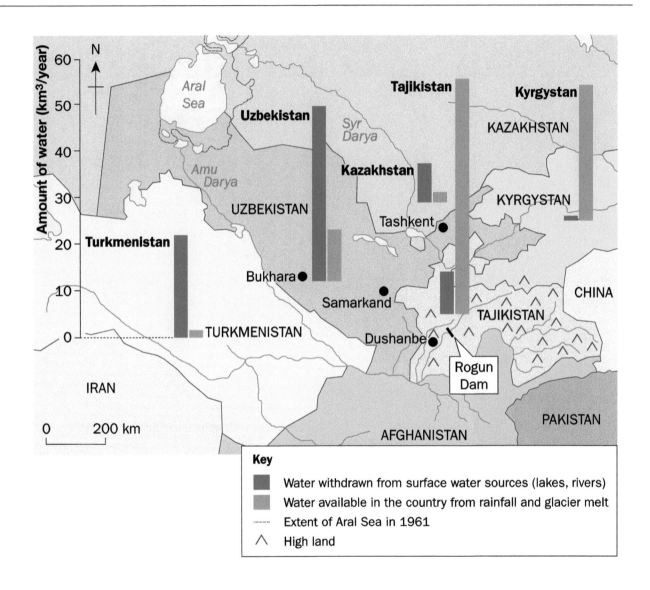

Key

Water withdrawn from surface water sources (lakes, rivers)

Water available in the country from rainfall and glacier melt

----- Extent of Aral Sea in 1961

∧ High land

Fig. 6 – A photograph showing part of Stoke Bishop in Bristol

**Fig. 7 – A graph showing the percentage of different crimes
committed over one year in Stoke Bishop**

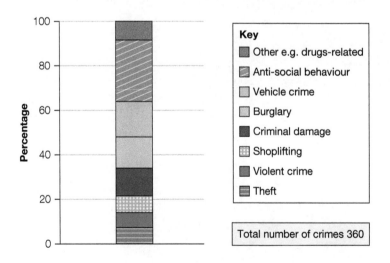

Key

- ■ Other e.g. drugs-related
- ▨ Anti-social behaviour
- ☐ Vehicle crime
- ☐ Burglary
- ■ Criminal damage
- ▦ Shoplifting
- ■ Violent crime
- ▤ Theft

Total number of crimes 360

Fig. 8 – A pie chart showing the percentage of crimes committed in Filwood over one year

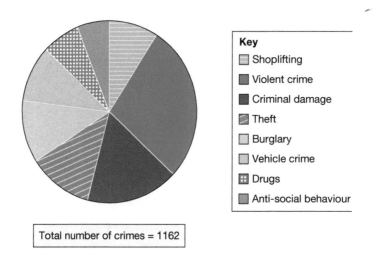

Key
- ☐ Shoplifting
- ■ Violent crime
- ■ Criminal damage
- ▨ Theft
- ☐ Burglary
- ☐ Vehicle crime
- ▦ Drugs
- ☐ Anti-social behaviour

Total number of crimes = 1162

Fig. 9 – A photograph of a street in Filwood

Fig. 10 – A bi-polar graph of environmental impact assessments taken in Filwood and Stoke Bishop in Bristol

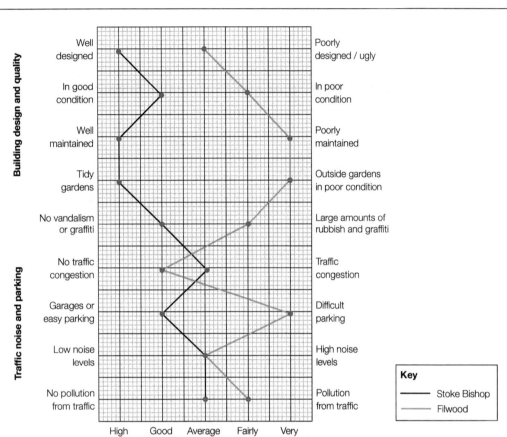

Fig. 11 – A map showing the location of two parts of Bristol where a human geography fieldwork investigation took place

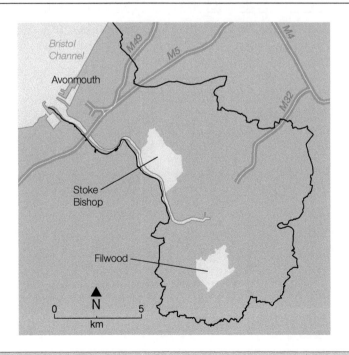

Fig. 1 – A graph showing the growth of the UK population

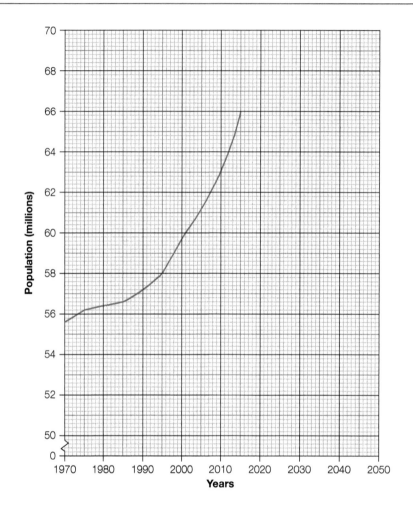

Fig. 2 – A map showing the percentage growth of the UK population, using census estimates, 2003–13

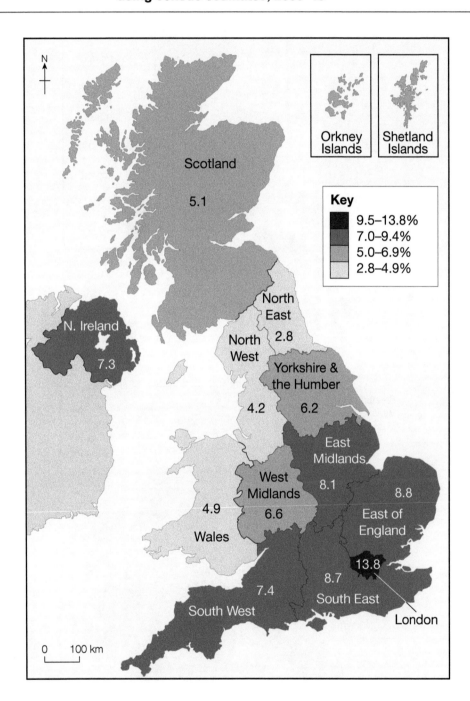

Fig. 3a – A map showing the annual population growth in Great Britain, 2012–14

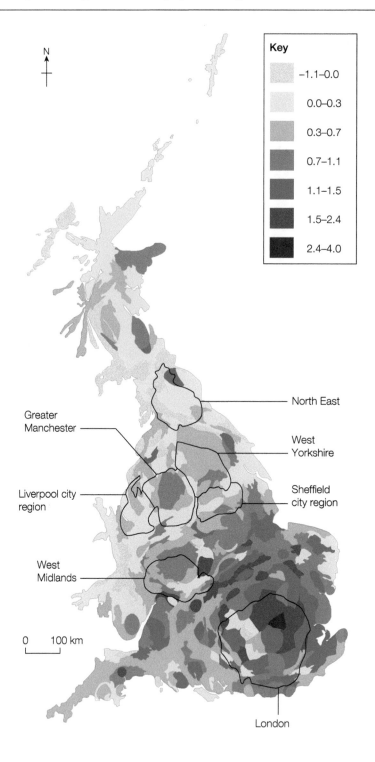

Key

	−1.1–0.0
	0.0–0.3
	0.3–0.7
	0.7–1.1
	1.1–1.5
	1.5–2.4
	2.4–4.0

North East

Greater Manchester

West Yorkshire

Liverpool city region

Sheffield city region

West Midlands

London

0   100 km

Fig. 3b – A map showing annual growth in housing in Great Britain, 2012–14

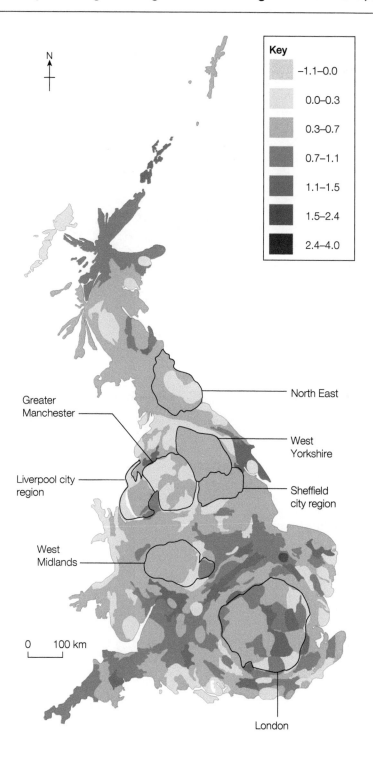

Key
- −1.1–0.0
- 0.0–0.3
- 0.3–0.7
- 0.7–1.1
- 1.1–1.5
- 1.5–2.4
- 2.4–4.0

N

North East

Greater Manchester

West Yorkshire

Liverpool city region

Sheffield city region

West Midlands

London

0   100 km

Fig. 4 – A map and graph showing the rising cost of housing in the UK

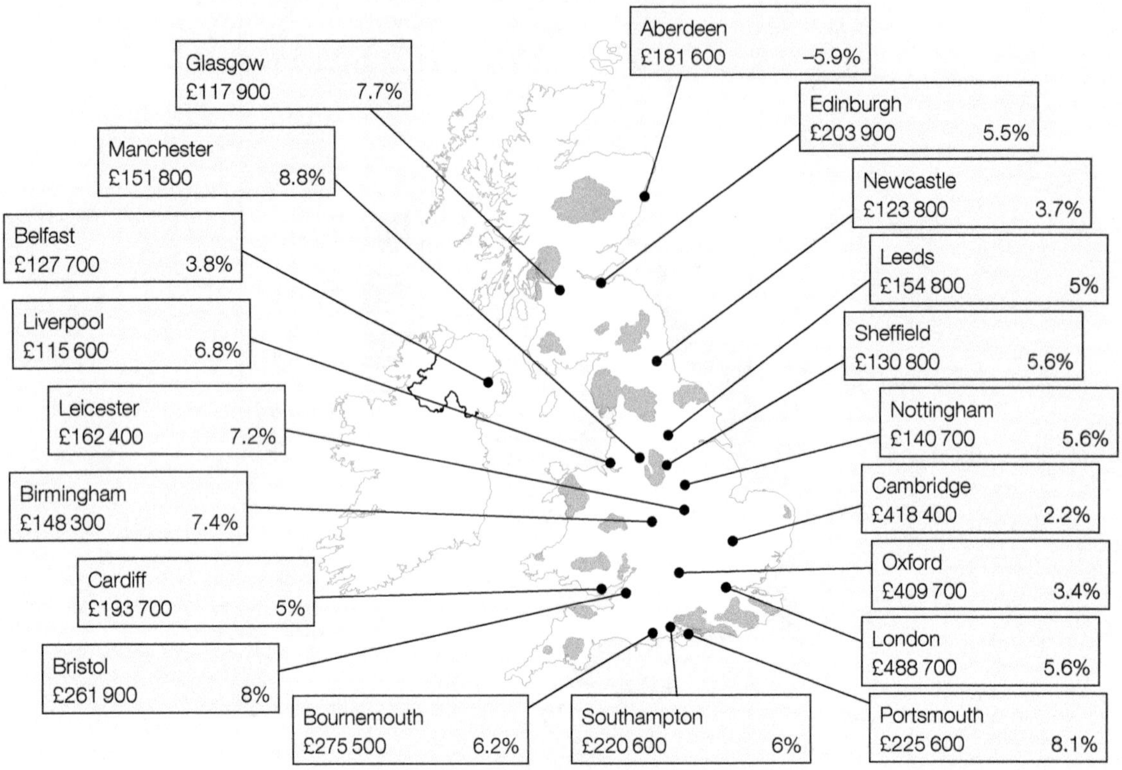
Aberdeen
£181 600 –5.9%
Glasgow
£117 900 7.7%
Edinburgh
£203 900 5.5%
Manchester
£151 800 8.8%
Newcastle
£123 800 3.7%
Belfast
£127 700 3.8%
Leeds
£154 800 5%
Liverpool
£115 600 6.8%
Sheffield
£130 800 5.6%
Leicester
£162 400 7.2%
Nottingham
£140 700 5.6%
Birmingham
£148 300 7.4%
Cambridge
£418 400 2.2%
Cardiff
£193 700 5%
Oxford
£409 700 3.4%
London
£488 700 5.6%
Bristol
£261 900 8%
Bournemouth
£275 500 6.2%
Southampton
£220 600 6%
Portsmouth
£225 600 8.1%

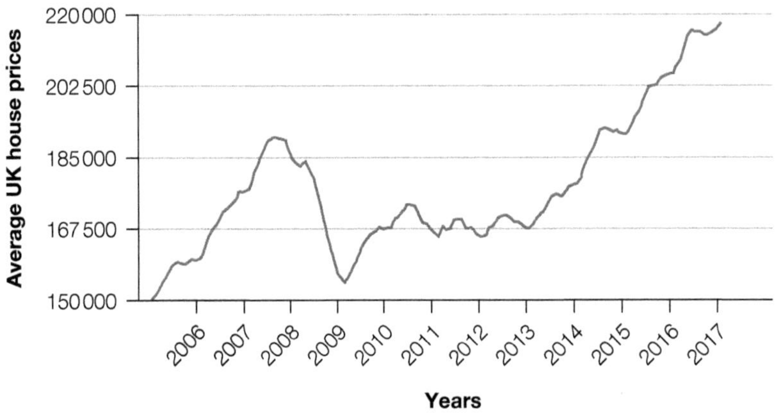
Average UK house prices
220000
202500
185000
167500
150000
2006
2007
2008
2009
2010
2011
2012
2013
2014
2015
2016
2017
Years

Fig. 5 – A graph showing the UK's housing shortage

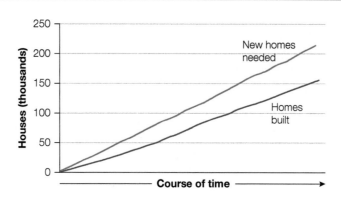

Fig. 6 – A factfile about changes in the UK population, 2000–15

Average life expectancy: males 85, rising to 87; females 91, rising to 94

Number of households: 23.7 million, rising to 27.2 million

Number of households with only one occupant: 6.6 million, rising to 7.7 million

Average age of first marriage: males 26 years, rising to 31 years; females 24 years, rising to 28 years

Net migration into the UK: 1% from EU and 3% from rest of the world, rising to 5% from EU and 4% from rest of the world

Fig. 7 – A bar chart showing the fastest growing cities in England

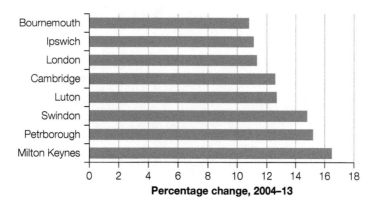

Fig. 8 – A map showing the main urban areas and green belts in England

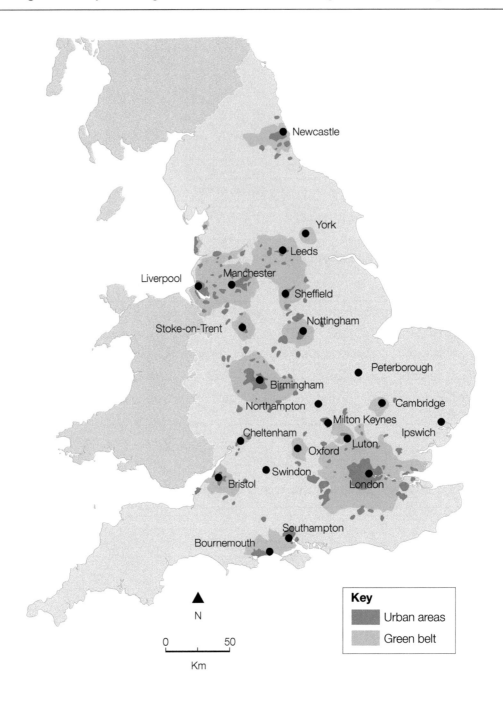

Fig. 9 – An extract from an OS map showing part of the green belt in Bristol

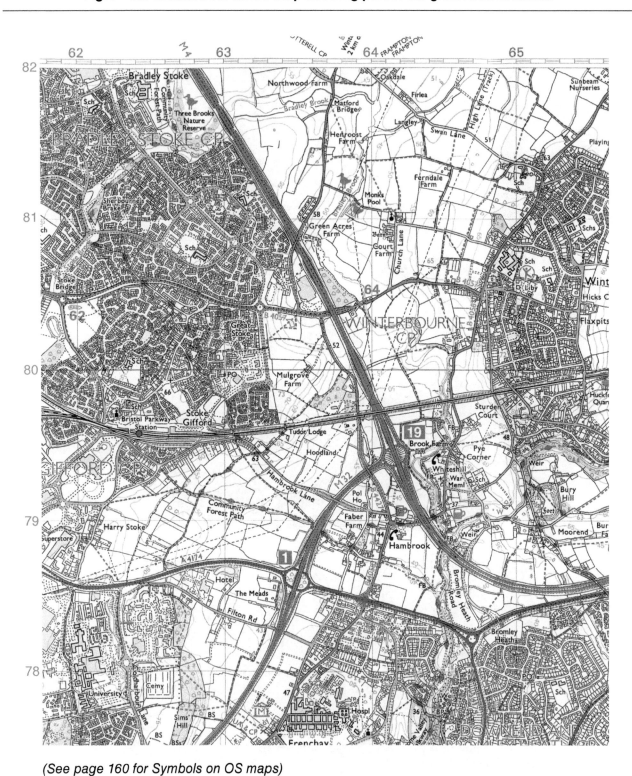

(See page 160 for Symbols on OS maps)

Figs 10a and 10b – Photographs showing disused industrial buildings in Bristol

---

Fig. 1 – A diagram showing a plate boundary

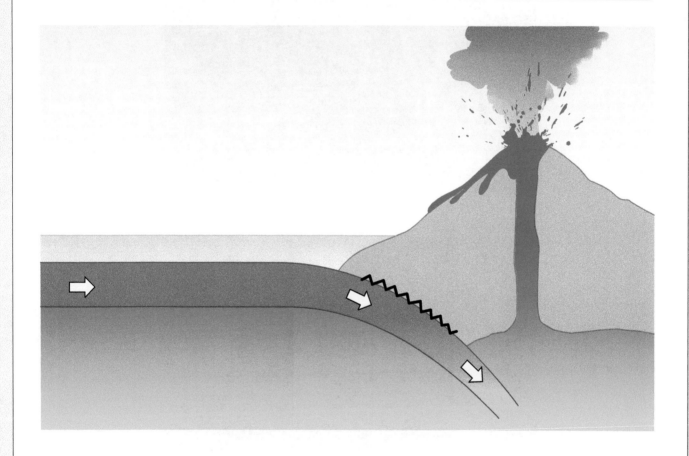

Fig. 2 – *Three photographs showing some impacts of climate change in the UK*

Fig. 3 – A diagram showing a coastal process

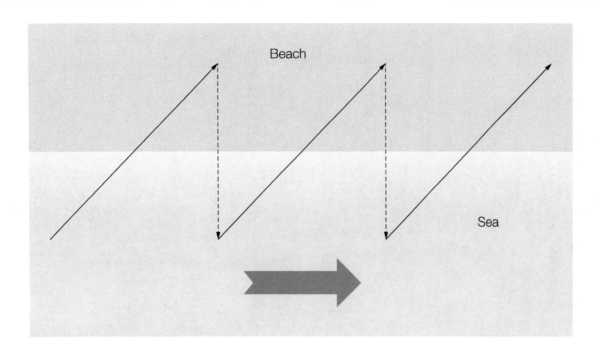

Beach

Sea

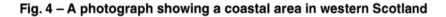

Fig. 4 – A photograph showing a coastal area in western Scotland

Fig. 5 – A photograph showing a pond ecosystem

Plants like reeds grow in the water around the edge of the pond.

On the banks grow grasses, bushes and trees.

At the edges of the pond, the water is shallow and there will be plants like water lilies.

On the surface are ducks and small insects such as water boatman.

At the centre water is deeper and there will be fish.

Fig. 6 – Two graphs showing the length (a) and shape (b) of river pebbles

---

a – Pebble length

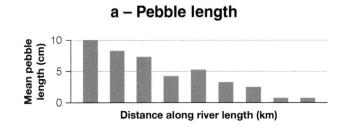

b – Pebble shape

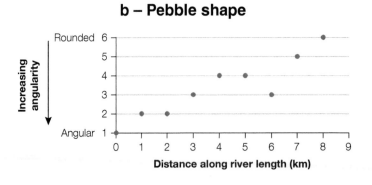

Fig. 1 – A photograph showing a city street scene in northern England

Fig. 2 – A location map showing Burkina Faso in Africa

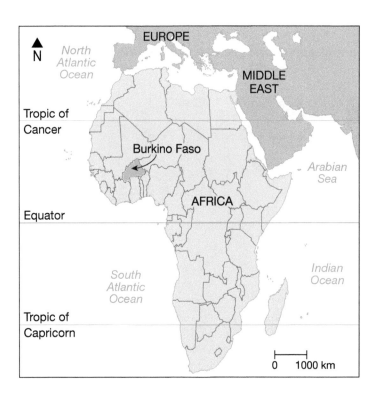

Fig. 3 – A factfile about Burkina Faso

- GNI (world ranking 164/188)
- HDI (world ranking 185/188)
- Surrounded by six countries
- Receives about 600–900 mm of rain per year
- Rainy season of 4 months or less
- Current environmental issues include: recent droughts and desertification severely affecting agricultural activities, overgrazing, soil degradation.
- 80% employed in agriculture
- 48% unemployment rate
- Succession of governments overthrown by force since gaining independence from France

Fig. 4 – A diagram of a population model

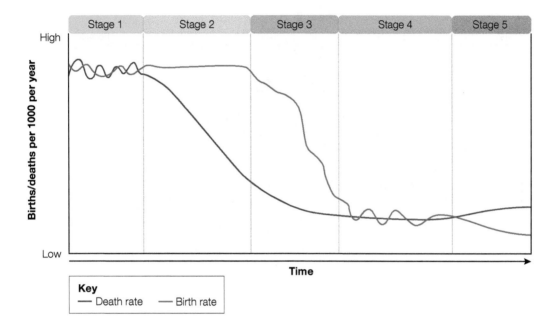

Figs 5a and 5b – Two population pyramids for the UK in 2001 and projected for 2021

a – 2001

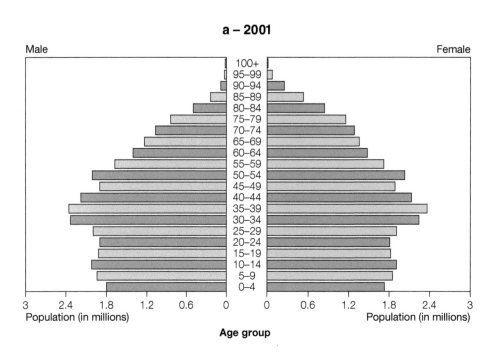

b – 2021

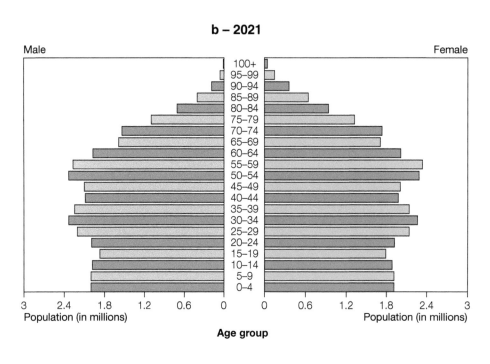

Fig. 6 – A map showing the percentage of the population aged over 65 in England and Wales

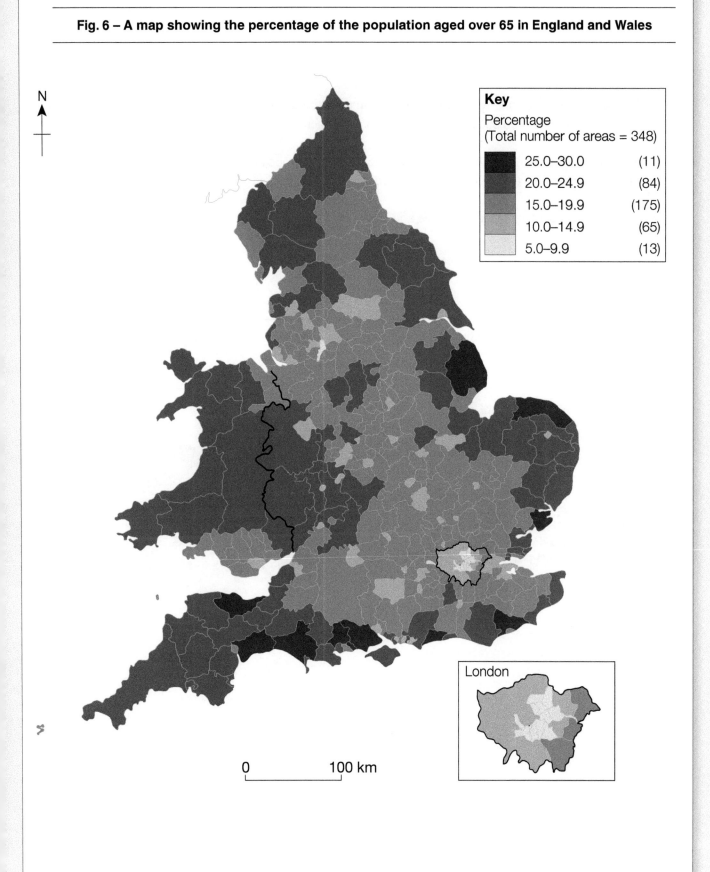

Key

Percentage
(Total number of areas = 348)

■	25.0–30.0	(11)
■	20.0–24.9	(84)
■	15.0–19.9	(175)
■	10.0–14.9	(65)
■	5.0–9.9	(13)

N

0   100 km

London

Fig. 7 – An extract from a newspaper article on the UK's ageing population

---

By the middle of the century, two million people in the UK will suffer from Alzheimer's, a form of dementia, with over 200 000 developing the condition each year.

The costs to the UK have increased to £26 billion a year. The people who are suffering from the disease, their carers and their families pay two-thirds of the costs.

The current cost of dementia diagnosis and treatment to the NHS is over £4 billion each year.

Fig. 8 – A world map showing average daily calorie consumption

---

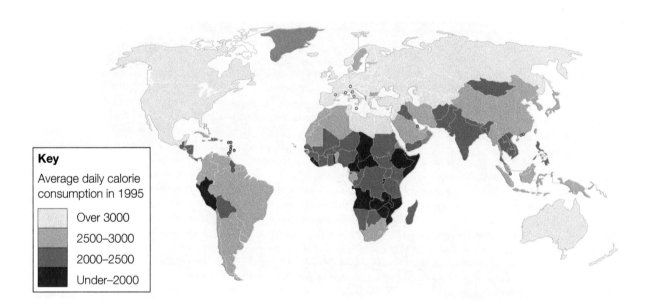

Key

Average daily calorie consumption in 1995

- Over 3000
- 2500–3000
- 2000–2500
- Under–2000

Fig. 9 – A cumulative frequency graph showing more results from the sphere of influence investigation

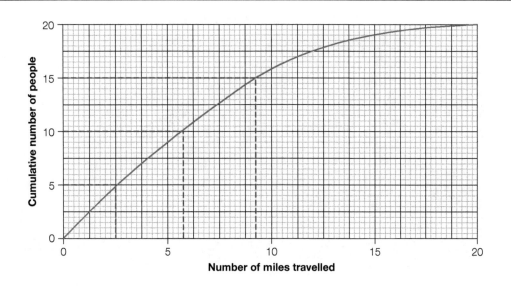

Figs 10a and 10b – Two pie graphs showing the results of a survey in different shopping areas

Shops in the Town Centre

Shops on the Retail Park

Figs 11a and 11b – Two photographs of the shopping centres

---

a – Town centre

b – Retail park

Fig. 12 – Results of a questionnaire survey

Questionnaire	Town centre		Retail park	
How far have you travelled to get to the shops?	Less than 1 mile	15	Less than 1 mile	3
	Between 1–5 miles	10	Between 1–5 miles	16
	Between 5–10 miles	5	Between 5–10 miles	22
	Over 10 miles	0	Over 10 miles	10
How long did you stay in the shopping area?	Less than an hour	4	Less than an hour	0
	Between 1–2 hours	16	Between 1–2 hours	7
	Between 3–4 hours	4	Between 3–4 hours	14
	More than 5 hours	1	More than 5 hours	9
How did you travel to get to the shops?	Walk	8	Walk	2
	Cycle	3	Cycle	0
	Car	9	Car	23
	Public transport	5	Public transport	5
Do you travel there just to shop or do you go for something else as well?	Yes	21	Yes	12
	No	4	No	18

Fig. 1 – A computer-generated image of a polar area

Fig. 2 – A graph showing average global temperatures based on recorded temperatures, 1880–2013

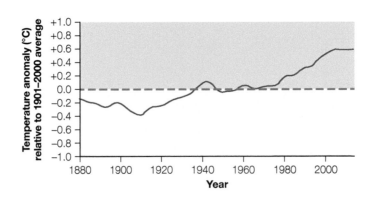

Fig. 3 – A photograph showing scientists working in the Arctic

---

Fig. 4 – Extracts from news articles about flooding in the UK

Tidal surge floods!

A tidal surge has hit the east coast of Britain, and it's the worst since the devastating floods of 1953, which killed hundreds. Thousand have been forced to abandon their homes as tides in parts of the North Sea reached the highest levels for 60 years.

Adapted from a BBC news extract, 6 December 2013

East coast towns flooded as tidal surge hits

There have been mass evacuations overnight along the east coast of the UK. Food defences, built to avoid a repeat of 1953, and flood warnings have given time for mass evacuation and saved many lives.

Adapted from a *Guardian* newspaper extract, 6 December 2013

Norfolk: the tidal surge and its impact on wildlife

Volunteers from groups such as the RSPB have said that nature reserves were affected by floods, with damage at the Snettisham reserve in Norfolk. Freshwater habitats have been inundated by salt water.

Adapted from a BBC news extract, 10 December 2013

Fig. 5 – A map and photograph showing Alkborough Flats

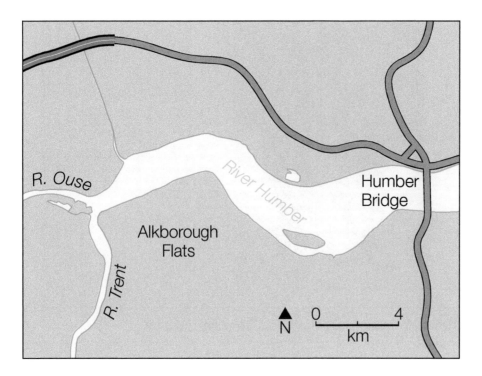

Fig. 6 – A factfile on the Alkborough Flats Tidal Defence Scheme

---

What did they do?
They:
- broke through the existing flood embankment creating a breach
- constructed channels to distribute the water, plus a spillway
- built a new flood bank to protect a sewage treatment plant and riding stables
- this means the sea can now flood the area at high tide.

Why did they do it?
It:
- provides a place to store flood water during extreme weather and high tides, reducing the possible flood level by 1.5 metres
- will reduce the risk of flooding to 300 000 properties
- creates a new wildlife habitat
- will encourage tourism, as a new visitor centre was built
- will help to adapt to climate change and rising sea levels

Fig. 7 – A map showing the location of the Maldives

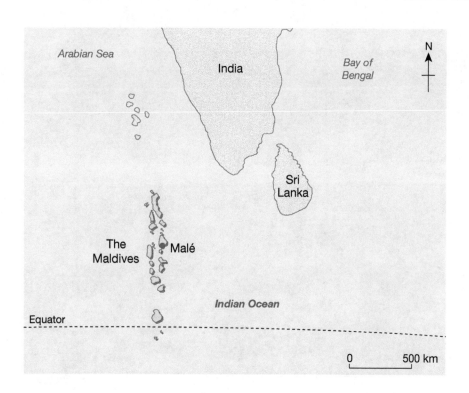

Fig. 8 – A factfile on the Maldives

- The Maldives is the lowest-lying country in the world.
- The 1000 km long island chain in the Indian Ocean has an average height of 1.5 metres. Its highest point is only 2.4 metres above sea level.
- The archipelago consists of 1200 islands, grouped into 26 coral atolls. Its total landmass represents just one-fifth the area of Greater London
- The islands lie on top of tall coral columns, which in turn are built on ancient underwater mountains.
- Globally coral reefs are the most endangered ecosystem.
- The population of almost 400 000 inhabits 200 islands but over a quarter of Maldivians live in the country's capital, Malé.
- Malé is the most densely populated city in the world with 110 000 people occupying two km^2 of land.

Fig. 9 – A computer-generated image of the Maldives shoreline

Fig. 10 – A graph showing different sectors of the Maldives' GDP

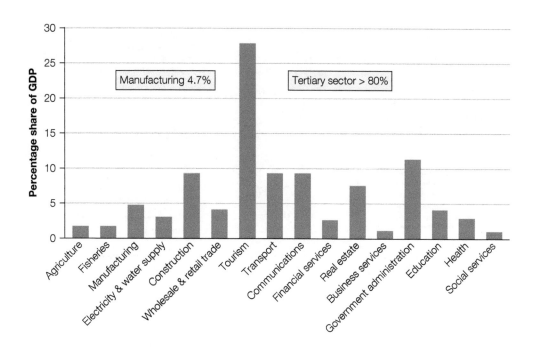

Manufacturing 4.7%

Tertiary sector > 80%

Fig. 11 – A table showing methods to reduce carbon emissions

Measure	Economic benefit (out of 12)	Climate benefit (out of 6)
Residential home energy efficiency	12	5
Public building energy efficiency	12	5
Boiler replacement programme	12	5
Light and appliance replacement	12	5
Fuel-efficient new cars	10	6
Renewable heat generation	10	5
Renewable energy development	9	6
Vehicle tyre pressure checks	11	4
Reducing deforestation	10	5

Fig. 12 – A map showing issues faced by the Maldives if the sea level continues to rise

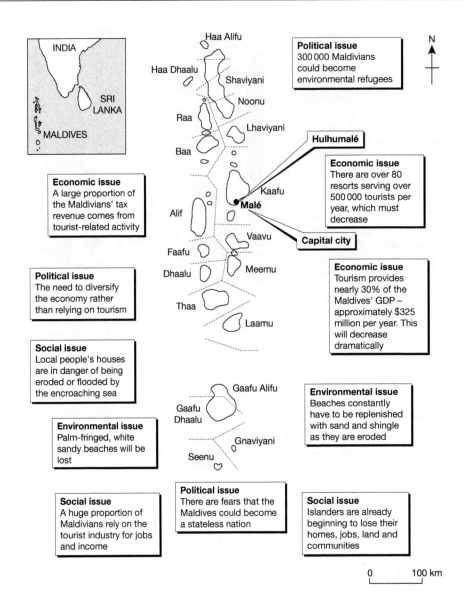

Fig. 13 – A photograph of Malé, the capital of the Maldives

Fig. 14 – A photograph of Hulhumalé, the new island being created in the Maldives

Hulhamalé

Seawalls, like those built around Malé, the capital (shown in **Fig. 13**), which are 3 metres high, may protect the city. However, building islands like Hulhamalé (shown above) may also be effective.

- The new city on Hulhamalé – called the City of Hope – will be over 2 metres above sea level and higher than the existing capital, Malé.
- Hulhamalé will rehouse 160 000 people and give the islanders 50 years more survival time.
- However, building the island involved dredging sand from the sea and covering the coral, which destroys the ecosystem and impacts on fishing.

Symbols on Ordnance Survey maps

ROADS AND PATHS

 Motorway — M1 or A 6(M)
Dual carriageway — A35
Trunk or main road — A31(T) or A35
Secondary road — B3074
Narrow road with passing places
Road under construction
Road generally more than 4 m wide
Road generally less than 4 m wide
Other road, drive or track, fenced and unfenced
Gradient: steeper than 1 in 5; 1 in 7 to 1 in 5
Ferry; Ferry P – passenger only
Path

PUBLIC RIGHTS OF WAY

(Not applicable to Scotland)

1:25 000	1:50 000	
		Footpath
		Road used as a public footpath
+++++++		Bridleway
		Byway open to all traffic

RAILWAYS

Multiple track
Single track
Narrow gauge/Light rapid transit system
Road over; road under; level crossing
Cutting; tunnel; embankment
Station, open to passengers; siding

BOUNDARIES

National
District
County, Unitary Authority, Metropolitan District or London Borough
National Park

HEIGHTS/ROCK FEATURES

Contour lines
·144 Spot height to the nearest metre above sea level

outcrop cliff scree

ABBREVIATIONS

P	Post office	PC	Public convenience (rural areas)
PH	Public house	TH	Town Hall, Guildhall or equivalent
MS	Milestone	Sch	School
MP	Milepost	Coll	College
CH	Clubhouse	Mus	Museum
CG	Coastguard	Cemy	Cemetery
Fm	Farm		

ANTIQUITIES

VILLA Roman
Castle Non-Roman
⚔ Battlefield (with date)
☆ Tumulus/Tumuli (mound over burial place)

LAND FEATURES

ruin Buildings
Public building
Bus or coach station
Place of Worship { with tower; with spire, minaret or dome; without such additions }
Chimney or tower
Glass structure
Ⓗ Heliport
△ Triangulation pillar
Mast
Wind pump / wind generator
Windmill
Graticule intersection
Cutting, embankment
Quarry
Spoil heap, refuse tip or dump
Coniferous wood
Non-coniferous wood
Mixed wood
Orchard
Park or ornamental ground
Forestry Commission access land
National Trust – always open
National Trust, limited access, observe local signs
National Trust for Scotland

WATER FEATURES

Marsh or salting
Towpath Lock Slopes Cliff High water mark
Aqueduct Canal Ford Flat rock Low water mark
Lighthouse (in use)
Weir Normal tidal limit Sand
Lake Bridge Dunes
Footbridge Lighthouse (disused)
Mud Shingle Beacon
Canal (dry)

TOURIST INFORMATION

Ⓟ Parking
P&R Park & Ride
Ⓥ Visitor centre
ℹ Information centre
📞 Telephone
Camp site/ Caravan site
Golf course or links
Viewpoint
PC Public convenience
Picnic site
Pub/s
Museum
Castle/fort
Building of historic interest
Steam railway
English Heritage
Garden
Nature reserve
Water activities
Fishing
Other tourist feature
Moorings (free)
Electric boat charging point
Recreation/leisure/ sports centre